Catholic to the Core!

Catholic to the Core!

Thoughts, Reflections, and Questions for Pastors, Parents, Administrators, and the Staff and Faculty of Today's Catholic Schools

KATHY HUSAK-TARNACKI

RESOURCE *Publications* · Eugene, Oregon

CATHOLIC TO THE CORE!
Thoughts, Reflections, and Questions for Pastors, Parents, Administrators, and the Staff and Faculty of Today's Catholic Schools

Resource Publications
An Imprint of Wipf and Stock Publishers
199 W. 8th Ave., Suite 3
Eugene, OR 97401

www.wipfandstock.com

PAPERBACK ISBN: 978-1-6667-3457-7
HARDCOVER ISBN: 978-1-6667-9058-0
EBOOK ISBN: 978-1-6667-9059-7

02/16/22

This book is lovingly dedicated to
My husband, Gerard

My children, Christopher, Emily, and Helene, and their
wonderful spouses Stephanie, Ryan, and Forrest

My precious grandchildren, Andrew, Abigail, Nicholas,
Nathaniel, Elizabeth, Leo, William, and Lucas

Your love and your lives inspire me and motivate me to pursue
God with all my heart.

I am so grateful for you and so proud of you all.

Contents

Acknowledgments

GRATITUDE (AS DEFINED BY Noah Webster in the *American Dictionary of the English Language 1828*)—an emotion of the heart, excited by a favor or benefit received.

My heart is filled with gratitude, emotion, and excitement as I complete this project which began seven years ago. It began merely as a prompting to put my thoughts down on paper. I had no idea of its purpose at the time. Now, with this wonderful opportunity for my words to go to print, I first thank Jesus. Since that life-changing day when I asked Him to take my heart into His hands, I have never been the same. There is not a day that goes by that I don't think about how blessed these years have been because of Him. Jesus has filled my life with hope in the midst of despair, comfort in the midst of sadness, courage in the midst of fear and struggle, healing in the midst of sickness, and joy in the midst of trials. My heart is filled with gratitude for His love and His presence in all circumstances. Every good gift I have received has been from above.

My husband Gerard is one of those amazing gifts. God brought us together at such a strategic time in both of our lives. He has been by my side for the past forty-three years. He has supported me, encouraged me, and stood by me through every joy, every challenge, and every sorrow. He has walked with me through many crazy ideas and out of ordinary pursuits. He has been my greatest cheerleader, always encouraging me to step out in the promptings of my heart, and always there to lend a hand to help me pursue my passions. He has prayed for me and loved me in ways I will never be able to repay fully. I am grateful beyond words for this extraordinary man—my husband.

Christopher, Emily, and Helene, I consider the privilege of being your mother another one of those greatest gifts. Each of you have grown into such amazing adults. At each stage of your lives I find myself feeling like I couldn't be more proud of you and it just couldn't get any better, but as each stage unfolds, that's exactly what has happened. You are incredible human beings and you continually give me more reasons to be proud and grateful as your mother. Thank you for the many ways your lives inspire me and challenge me to reach higher and try to live my life in ways that leaves no room for regrets.

Stephanie, Ryan, and Forrest, you entered our family through marriage, but it feels as though you have been here from the beginning. God couldn't have brought anyone more perfectly suited for my children than each of you are. Thank you for the love, joy, and strength you bring into this family and for making me feel more like "mom" than a mother-in-law.

My precious grandchildren, Andrew, Abigail, Nicholas, Nathaniel, Elizabeth, Leo, William, Lucas—you melt my heart and inspire me to continue to pursue God's very best! You are a beautiful reflection of God's grace, and the simplicity and purity of your love for Jesus fills me with gratitude and joy, and most importantly with hope! You are the face of a generation that I pray will be on fire for the Lord—a generation that will not compromise and will not settle for anything less than fulfilling God's amazing plans and purposes. I pray every day that you will pursue your God-given destiny with great passion and fervor and that you will help others do the same.

Though they are no longer living, I thank God for my parents and for the way they filled my childhood with the beauty and gift of faith and family. My passions are a result of the beautiful ways those early years impacted my life. I am grateful for my siblings Julie, Mary Jane, Dave, and Mickey for the many ways they have influenced my life and helped shape me into who I am today.

Acknowledgments

I am a very blessed woman, and I thank God for this incredible opportunity to publish this book and trust that any good that it may accomplish will be because of Him and His precious gifts.

How This Book Came to Be

WRITING A BOOK WAS really never anything I thought I would do. My life was full with family responsibilities and the time commitments in my different roles as a teacher and administrator. But once I found myself with time away from administrative responsibilities, I felt a desire and prompting to put into words thoughts and reflections resulting from a very unique journey of faith and education.

From the time I was a little girl I wanted to be a teacher. I imagined that one day I would really have my own classroom. I loved being in my little Ukrainian Catholic school and loved the Sisters and teachers that I had. I loved Jesus and thought at times that maybe someday I would be a nun, but then I moved on to high school and I found myself very confused about my future and my faith.

Being in a Roman Catholic high school in the 1970s proved to be very unsettling for me. Having been raised in a very traditional Byzantine Catholic background I became bewildered as the Catholic Church in America was sorting through and making changes based on interpretations from the Second Vatican Council. In my particular situation it seemed the lines became blurred and the teachings of the Church became unclear. It was a time in our society of increasing promiscuity, frequent drinking (as the drinking age was lowered to eighteen), heavy drug use, etc. Religion classes were no longer opportunities to learn tenets of faith, but rather opportunities to search and delve into who we were by listening to and interpreting music such as Simon and Garfunkel's "I Am a Rock," and learning about world religions. As the drug use and drinking increased, so did casual sex and the use of abortion as a possible form of birth control. I knew that "those in charge" in my Catholic school and the Church at large must know this is going on! Why wasn't it being addressed, why were we as young people being left to our own devices, and ultimately I began to wonder if the Church had a stand anymore or if it was changing its course. It was at this point I began to feel somewhat lukewarm in my faith. I never stopped attending Mass and still had a love for Christ and His church in my heart, but it had grown cool and lacking in fervor. I wasn't sure where to look or how to reach out for direction. There didn't seem to be any. So I did what so many other people did at that time—I just went through the motions.

I went on to a public university and began to pursue a degree in elementary education. I loved my courses, loved my student teaching, and found fulfillment in feeling that I was doing something worthwhile. Being the youngest of five children and the only one in the family to complete a college education I felt I had accomplished much. I secured a teaching position in a public elementary school, I married a wonderful man, started a family, and just kept moving along—all the while knowing deep in my heart that something was missing. Due to millage issues my position was eliminated and I moved on to teach at a well-established Catholic elementary school. Again it seemed something was missing. We went to Mass weekly and had religion classes but my heart still felt dull. My students didn't appear any more excited than I was. Was it just me or was something really missing? I couldn't put my finger on it so I just kept going through the motions and tried to fill the void through "good things"—healthy eating, creating a good home for our family, eventually leaving teaching to be a full-time mother. It seemed to help, but I would always come back to that void.

But then, someone stepped into my life and changed it forever. It was a woman named Anne, a neighbor who would babysit for me occasionally. She was a "born-again" Christian woman and she had something I wanted. She was gentle, kind, and secure in her faith. There was a peace and confidence she carried with her. She made it known that she prayed, and that she prayed for me. She never pushed her faith; she just gently lived it. She would leave me little prayers and notes of encouragement. Sometimes to help me as a young mother she would suggest I tune into Dr. James Dobson and his radio show, "Focus on the Family." At first I felt nervous about this "Christian" stuff because Catholics were Catholics and Christians were usually "Protestants" and in my life the two didn't cross paths very often. But then something in my heart began to soften and stir. I began to appreciate her heartfelt prayers (sometimes praying for me before she left my house) and her sincere suggestions. I began to listen to Dr. Dobson and began to look for books about being a Christian woman and mom. It was as if something dormant was coming to life within me. I began to hunger for more and wanted to keep digging and talking about what I was experiencing, and for sure I began to make my wonderful husband a little nervous about this newfound faith in his wife! Being the amazing man that he is, he patiently listened and withheld any concerns he may have had.

It's very frustrating to have this excitement building in your heart, and at the same time feel like I was in the midst of a fog. Though still Catholic, attending Mass every week, I found myself frustrated. The people around me were doing what I had done for years—simply going through the motions. Now I recognized it, where before I was doing the same thing and couldn't see it. Something was pulling at me to be alive, yet so much around me seemed dry—lacking life.

So for a couple more years, we stayed on the surface of this newfound faith. We tried different things, but didn't get very far trying it alone. Then, we made a move to a quaint little town in Michigan (still partially pursuing that idyllic home and setting to raise a family). We put our home up for sale and bought an old historic home and became excited about living in this small town. Without taking too much space by sharing all the details, I will simply say the bottom dropped out on us. The sale on the home we previously lived in fell through, we now owned this new home that needed a lot of work, had two mortgages on one income (I was no longer working), and my husband's straight-commission job was experiencing the stress of the economy and his paychecks were much smaller. It truly was the most frightening time in our lives. We questioned everything—our faith, our decisions, what to do with our future. On a very desperate day, I knew I had to call someone for support, and of course the first person to come to mind was Anne—the neighbor with faith. She prayed with me on the phone and assured me we were right where God wanted us. She encouraged me to get into a women's Bible study for strength and support. Though I had never read the Bible (in my experience growing up, Catholics didn't do that—only Protestants did) I knew she was right. In God's great goodness—wouldn't you know, right after that recommendation from Anne, I stepped outside, where within minutes a neighbor invited me to a new women's Bible study that had just started! Never having had experiences like that before, I knew in my heart that God was reaching out to me, meeting me right where I was, trying to urge me towards Him. Not only did this group have a women's Bible study, but the men met weekly also. My husband and I then knew we were going to be okay and it was time for us to let go and turn our lives completely over to Christ. Though space limits my ability to fully share all that took place, I will say it was an amazing time in our lives. It was like a door had been unlocked and light was let in. Our marriage became fuller, our family more Christ-centered. Our choices in entertainment, music, everything, changed—and it was good. But . . . it led us away from our Catholic roots (We had been evangelized by people who were now our friends, but were not Catholic, although most of them were ex-Catholics). At first we would attend their nondenominational church and also attend Mass, but slowly Mass was phased out and we became fully committed to this new evangelical Christian church. We loved it and we loved the people. They were like family, and we spent a lot of time together. We shared faith, encouraged one another in marriage and family life, prayed together, and most importantly we grew to know and love Jesus in a more profound, deeper way. We became a part of the leadership team of the church, ran the Sunday School program, my husband ran the men's ministry and I opened a Christian school on the church campus where I was able to create and plan a K–8 curriculum that was completely Christ-centered and academically rich. Eventually we were ordained elders and considered associate pastors. We stepped in occasionally to preach at a Sunday service, taught at men's and women's retreats and thought this would be home for many years to come. Our faith life was more vibrant and alive than it had ever been and we couldn't imagine ever leaving.

Then it was time for our fist child, our son, to attend high school. Having had the experience of such a rich atmosphere of faith and education, we were torn with what to do for high school. There was no Christian high school anywhere nearby and his class-mates were all going to attend the public high school, which was literally two blocks from our house. My husband and I made an un-announced visit to the public high school and our hearts sank. The stark difference between what he had experienced up to this point and what existed there left us knowing we had to find something else. Ironically, people thought we were crazy for looking, feeling that if they all went to this public high school together they could support one another and they would be fine. But after much prayer we knew in our hearts that God was leading us elsewhere, so we became determined to find what "elsewhere" was. With very few options, out of the blue my husband recommended a Catholic high school about thirty-five miles away! He had heard about this school in his travels in sales. We visited, prayed, and discerned that this was the place. Despite baffled friends who couldn't understand why in the world we would enroll our son in a Catholic school after leav-ing the Catholic Church—we did. And from that decision our lives began another very challenging journey. As we experienced the at-mosphere of a Catholic high school again, now with hearts forever changed, our faith alive and vibrant, we began to see with new eyes and understand things about the Catholic faith that we never did before. By the time our middle child began her high-school years (two years later) we knew something in our hearts was shifting and God was preparing us for another change in our course. Our Catholic roots began to take on new life and we began to hunger for truth regarding the Catholic faith. We were at a crossroads and had to know God's will clearly. So without sharing anything with our church family we spent the next two years praying and studying the Catholic faith. We had to know and understand what we had left in the Catholic faith before we could make another huge, life-changing decision. It didn't take long for us to realize that God was calling us home to the Catholic Church, but He was calling us back as new individuals—ones who clearly understood what it means to have a personal relationship with Jesus and who now knew their Catholic faith in a way they were never taught before.

It was exciting and heartbreaking at the same time, for now we knew we had to step down from our leadership positions and begin the process of leaving the church and friends we had grown to love over eighteen years. It was one of the most difficult steps to date that we have had to take. We hung on to the hope that despite our decision, the relationships built would last. Unfortunately that was not the case. Additionally, in the midst of taking this step I was hit with very troubling news regarding my health and was referred to a surgeon for what was suspected to be ovarian cancer—a cancer which I was told, once discovered, is generally in stages too late to cure. The ultrasounds and blood tests supported the concern and I was scheduled for a complete hysterectomy with an oncologist present for the steps that would have to follow. Needless to say I was devastated and confused and couldn't understand why, in the midst of calling us back to the Catholic faith, God would allow me to face this life-threatening situation. But in the center of the fear was a peace that He was with me, confirmed by my husband's faithful prayers and love for me. I had to trust Him and just keep taking one step after another. Five days before my surgery—urged by my brother—my husband and I traveled to the Solanus Casey Center in Detroit to receive prayer at the tomb of Solanus Casey. A feeble priest prayed for me (not once asking what I was seeking prayer for), heard my confession and shuffled away. My hopes of a "word" regarding my situation never came—and I just had to trust. Then on the way home we drove to a church in Wyandotte, Michigan—urged by my sister—where a priest from Chicago was holding a healing Mass. I went up and received prayer, and as others were receiving words of healing and hope and were slain in the spirit—I had nothing happen. I went back to my pew—again trying to just trust. Two days before the surgery, my husband and I went to my doctor's appointment to sign papers and get instructions for the surgery. My husband, the man of great faith that he is, requested one more ultrasound. Though the doctor felt it was unnecessary since I had had so many and each time the growth was larger, she agreed hesitantly. To her great surprise the growth had decreased to half the size. She sent me to the lab, stating that if the numbers were the same, we had to proceed with surgery. Again to her surprise, the number she was tracking had dropped by ten points! She cancelled the surgery and had me back in two weeks to discover that the growth was completely gone! Was it the prayers of Solanus Casey or the healing priest from Chicago, or the prayers of my family or children? For now, I can't know—but for sure, I know God's hand was in wherever it came from! What a gift from God in the midst of the tumultuous transition. We proceeded with our entry back into the Catholic Church, and we were welcomed back, went to Confession, and received the Eucharist for the first time in a long time by Fr. Racca at the Basilica of the Sacred Heart at the University of Notre Dame, where our son was a student. Less than a year later we sold our house in that quaint historical town and moved to Jackson, Michigan, where God amazingly opened a door for me to serve as a Catholic school principal.

I couldn't believe how God had orchestrated every detail of our lives, blessed us in so many ways, and now was allowing me to take all those experiences and bring them into Catholic education. What a joy and privilege—though it certainly was not easy! Imagine an on-fire, Holy Spirit-filled revert to the faith, stepping into a Catholic school that had become very much like so many other Catholic schools—academic institutions with a touch of faith here and there. For the first few years I was met with suspicion, skepticism, and at times very strong opposition. I had learned so much through all my previous experiences about persevering and trusting that I felt God had given me what I needed to face this battle. At times, it was quite a battle, but after a few years the culture of the school changed, the hearts of the children grew so tender and sensitive to faith, and we were blessed with an amazing Eucharistic Adoration blessing (I call it a miracle) where the face of Jesus appeared on the Blessed Sacrament in the monstrance on one of our First Friday All-School Adoration Days. But that's another story!

After five years at this school I felt God's call to a new work—a new all-girl's Catholic high school with a mission to educate young women according to the teachings of Pope John Paul II on the dignity and vocation of women. High school—something else I had never done, but as I trusted in God's grace He provided me with what I needed to oversee its early years of development, an accreditation, and the development of a complete high school program.

Now as a new grandmother, I have taken time to step away from the responsibilities of running a school to enjoy this new great blessing in my life and to reflect back on all that God has done for me, shown me, and allowed me the privilege to experience. All of it—the joys, sorrows, accomplishments, and failures—is what leads me to write this book.

A vibrant, genuine, Catholic education should be one of the greatest gifts available to a child. It should be filled with truth, life, joy, peace, strength, comfort, wisdom, and all the spiritual and academic tools necessary to face the challenges of our very secular, confused culture. But unfortunately many of our Catholic schools are barely any different than our public schools—though they may have Mass occasionally, crucifixes on the wall, and a weak collection of religion classes. Sometimes I fear that environment is even more dangerous to the souls of our young, because it fools them and their parents into believing they have something they don't—TRUTH!

This is why I am writing this book. I am very humbled by the journey Christ has allowed me to take, the experiences He has exposed me to, and the opportunities He has given me to know Him and love Him more deeply as the years have passed. The path hasn't been a typical one. There were many detours and unexpected twists and turns, but God was there in it all! As Fr. Racca said to me when I expressed sadness that I had lost all those years in the Catholic Church, "God writes straight with our crooked lines." I don't claim to have all the answers or to have done things perfectly (or in a conventional way) in my different situations, but I do know that I have grown from each and every experience. I discovered aspects of faith that perhaps I may never have found had we not been on that particular course. I believe God has given me a unique perspective as a cradle Catholic who grew lukewarm, to an on-fire evangelical Christian, to a very grateful, Holy Spirit-filled revert to the Catholic faith—as a teacher in public education to lukewarm Catholic education as both a teacher and principal to a time where Pope John Paul II's teachings on The New Evangelization is beginning to bubble up and impact our seminaries, our churches, and our schools. I know that each and every experience as we grow in our faith has a purpose and is meant to be shared and that's what I hope to do through this book.

The message is very simple, sometimes very direct, but the execution of it all can be very challenging in this culture. I am hoping that as I draw from my unique background and share principles of faith that I have discovered and believe can make our Catholic schools more genuine, that perhaps someone will try them out and find them to be life giving and helpful. What I will share may contain some practical things I have found to be helpful, but primarily will be principles of faith that are not mine but are from God's word and from church teaching—principles that can definitely change a culture and promotes strength, unity, and a lasting foundation upon which to build for years to come. The future depends upon the education of our young and to educate them without vibrant faith is to poorly educate them.

> The Christian ideal has not been tried and found wanting. It has been found difficult; and left untried.
>
> That is the one eternal education:
> to be sure enough that something is true
> that you dare to tell it to a child.
>
> Education is only truth in a state of transmission.
>
> —G. K. Chesterton

If we do not agree on the truth, how can we teach it to our children?

Who Do You Say That I Am?

And it happened that while He was praying alone, the disciples were with Him, and He questioned them, saying, "Who do the people say that I am?" They answered and said, "John the Baptist, and others say Elijah; but others, that one of the prophets of old has risen again." And He said to them, "But who do you say that I am?"

—Luke 9:18–20 (RSV)

"Who do you say that I am?" is THE critical question. As a Catholic, in a sense, that was the question asked at our baptism—answered by our parents and godparents. It is what we need to ask ourselves continually, and certainly at the beginning, all throughout, and at the end of every venture, every decision, and then finally as we end our lives. It is the question that, if answered honestly and sincerely, will cause us to evaluate what we really believe and how willing we are to stand for that belief. In a culture which continues to become more and more secular and separated from God, the challenges associated with our faith increase. From being a country founded on faith, we now are being hushed in every area. Not only is Christianity being formally removed from just about everything, but positions that are clearly opposed by the Catholic Church are now gaining acceptance and admittance, and any stated opposition is considered hateful and discriminatory.

Background research, as discussed in an articles from Catho-liCity, indicates:

> By 2010, based on our research, including reviews of decades worth of polling bolstered by professional inter-action with tens of thousands of Catholics, we estimate that fewer than five percent of Catholics in the United States believe and practice what the Church teaches as the Church herself teaches it. This tiny minority makes up a minority of the 20 percent of baptized Catholics who still regularly attend Sunday Mass.
>
> These statistics can vary greatly depending on the diocese and parish, but of the roughly fifteen million Catholic families in the United States, we estimate that there remain only 150,000 families raising children under the age of eighteen who live in accord with the magisterial teachings of the Church—or a handful of families or fewer per parish. These families consider be-ing devoutly Catholic the unparalleled purpose of life.[1]

Staggering statistics! Now that we are well beyond 2010, we can only imagine how much further we have moved in the wrong direction. How did we get from where we were to where we are now? I believe that if we return to the question, "Who do YOU say that I am?" we can find the answer. For it is in the individual answers to this question that the course of our nation has been de-termined. You see, it wasn't enough that our country was founded on Christian principles. Those principles last only as long as there are individuals to uphold them, to sacrifice for them, and at times give their life for them. It is up to each and every one of us to answer the question personally, then to form community with others who have asked and answered the same question definitively for them-selves. It cannot be answered or maintained by riding on someone else's coattail of faith. Jesus was making this point very clear in the above Scripture as He asked His disciples that question. First He asked them what "everyone else" was saying about Him, to which the disciples had a variety of answers (John the Baptist, Elijah, prophets, etc.). It is still a very pertinent question today. If Jesus

1. McFarlane, "Bright Future," 3.

was here and asked it again, the answers would still be numerous (a prophet, a great teacher, etc.), not to mention the myriad of definitions you would get for Christianity, faith, religion, etc. In asking that question, first Jesus sets the stage, causing them to state out loud that "out there" the answer is unclear and varied. THEN Jesus asks the big question, "WHO DO YOU SAY THAT I AM?" because it doesn't matter what is said "out there." What matters is what is happening in me first. What do I believe? Who and what do I trust? What am I willing to stand for? Who is Jesus in MY life? These were the questions I had to face as an adult who had been influenced through the years by all that was "out there." It was the question that I never heard (either because I wasn't listening or because it wasn't being asked) in my Catholic church. Instead I heard it for the first time indirectly from a neighbor named Anne, and then directly from a group of evangelical Christians—many of which, ironically, had been raised Catholic themselves. I heard it in a place removed from where I grew up (approximately 150 miles away), where I could investigate and dig without the disappointment or disapproval of Catholic family and friends. It was new territory and I could traverse it freely. The rubber hit the road for me. Lukewarm, going-through-the-motions faith had become unsettling. It lacked conviction and depth, and I was experiencing what St. Augustine describes when he said, "Thou hast made us for thyself, O Lord, and our heart is restless until it finds its rest in thee."[2]

In my Spirit I wanted something worth defending—I wanted TRUTH, and I was grateful for the boldness of Anne and my evangelical friends for asking the important question. This is not to diminish the efforts or the faith of family and friends. It just became clear that they couldn't carry me. It was time for me to take responsibility and decide where I was headed, because that decision would determine everything going forward.

After much wrestling I let go and asked JESUS to take over my life. It occurred one morning as I was getting ready for my day. After much internal wrestling I finally let go and made a decision. In essence I was answering with the apostles—"You are the Christ,"

2. Augustine, *Confessions*, 1, 1–2, 2.5, 5.

and I want you to be the center of my life! In evangelical circles they call it "being saved" or "born again," and honestly, even though I was raised to believe in Jesus, I was being saved—saved from myself and a lukewarm, half-hearted faith. From that moment my heart was lifted of a burden. I was excited and felt alive like never before. And, in God's amazing grace and goodness, my husband had the same experience THAT DAY in his car while traveling around making sales calls. What a gift that we made that decision the same day! And you see—we didn't make it sitting together in a room. We each made it ON OUR OWN without the other person knowing, and AFTER making the decision by ourselves, we could come together and begin to build a life of faith for our marriage and family just as, once each disciple made his personal decision, they could together build the church!

So what about you? Where are you in the process? Were you raised in faith and then found it was hard to make your own as an adult? Were you influenced by our secular culture of materialism and individualism and now find yourself afraid you will have to give up too much? Was faith barely present in your childhood years or did something happen in your life that left you doubting and questioning your faith? Are you afraid of being ridiculed, tossed aside, left behind or left alone? I struggled with all the above and to my great surprise, I only gained—I never felt I lost anything. You see, when we give God everything, He gives us way more than we give up—and the giving up is actually a relief and many times a joy. After that day I gained peace, joy, happiness, courage, strength, hope, and on and on . . . I let go of things freely. My choice in entertainment changed, my discernment in music clarified. I still remember early on after this happened, walking the aisles of my local grocery store singing along to a song I had always enjoyed and found myself shocked at the words I was actually singing. Though I still liked my 1960s oldies, Christian music began to touch my heart and spirit in ways that brightened my days and enlarged my faith. I found that creating a home that was joyful, faith-filled, wholesome, pure, and Christ-centered became a desire and focus. Protecting and nurturing the development of faith within our home became my number-one priority. I wanted to make sure my children had every opportunity to make the decision I had made, for I now knew nothing else mattered nearly as much.

Did everything become easy? No, absolutely not! We faced many challenges—health, finances, relationships, etc., but we now faced them with hope and trust that either God was using them to develop and strengthen us or they were simply challenges of life that He would see us through while providing for every need.

As a Catholic educator—whether you are a teacher, administrator, secretary, parent—it doesn't matter. You have a responsibility as one bearing the name of "Catholic educator" to have decided to make Jesus the center of your life, to know your faith, to love your faith, to be willing to defend your faith, so that the next generation can have a chance, can witness the joy and peace of a life lived in Christ. They deserve our best, our fullest, our sincerest, and most genuine efforts. To provide anything less continues the domino effect of allowing the culture to be the loudest, clearest voice. I would even go so far to say that if you can't make this commitment you shouldn't be in Catholic education. There are many charter schools and public schools that would welcome and value your professional talents. Catholic schools need faithful, on-fire Catholic educators. They need teachers and administrators who look at everything through a lens of faith—every lesson, every policy and procedure, every discipline method—a group of people committed to building a community of faith, hope, and love. Children need teachers who naturally have a perspective of faith always flowing, teachers who don't require a list of Scriptures to be given to them to integrate faith into their subject matter because they are men and women who read Scripture and have it flowing naturally from them—not artificially from someone else's lists or plans.

I'm not suggesting "perfect" faith-filled educators—what I am suggesting is that our children, our Catholic schools, need educators who want truth, who want Jesus to be the center of their lives; educators who sincerely love the Catholic faith, and though they may have a lot to learn, they want to learn. What an awesome journey for a classroom filled with children to witness students and teacher digging into the faith, looking into Scripture, finding truth and answers to questions prevalent in todays world.

It all begins with the question, "Who do YOU say that I am?" and a heart open and willing to take the risk of letting Christ have control! So where are you in this journey? Wherever you are, are you ready and willing to take the next step, and the next one— each day allowing Christ to change you, soften you, mold you, and shape you? Because if you say yes, He will give you all you need, personally and professionally.

Each day we get up and we nourish our bodies with food and drink. Why is it that our time with God, our time in prayer and studying His word, becomes something so easily neglected, put aside for other things? We don't allow much time to pass when our body is hungry before feeding it, but we often let our starving souls continue to starve. And the truth is that God won't force us—even though He knows how desperately we need Him. He desires that we choose to say yes, that we choose to get to know Him, that we choose to embrace His Truth and live a life that honors and glorifies Him. He wants a loving relationship with you, a relationship built on trust and hope and joy so that He can be there at our side, helping us realize the most meaningful life possible.

If you are fearful of what taking a step like this will mean in your life, doubtful it will work out, anxious you will fail, etc., may I say that this is all normal. Because as sure as there is a God who loves you, there is a devil who wants nothing more than the ruin of your soul. He will minister doubt, fear, anxiety—whatever will hold you back. But once you take that step, make that decision to allow Christ to reign in your heart, you will never regret it, and a peace that transcends your understanding will overshadow your doubts and fears.

> It is Jesus that you seek when you dream of happiness;
> He is waiting for you when nothing else you find satisfies
> you; He is the beauty to which you are so attracted; it is
> He who provoked you with that thirst for fullness that
> will not let you settle for compromise; it is He who urges
> you to shed the masks of a false life; it is He who reads in

your heart your most genuine choices, the choices that others try to stifle. It is Jesus who stirs in you the desire to do something great with your lives, the will to follow an ideal, the refusal to allow yourselves to be ground down by mediocrity, the courage to commit yourselves humbly and patiently to improving yourselves and society, making the world more human and more fraternal.[3]

How do you take this step? Get quiet before the Lord; begin to sincerely have a conversation with Him. Tell Him your fears, your desires, ask Him to forgive you for boxing Him out, let Him know that you want His will and His ways, and ask Him to take over your life! Then after you have taken that step—if you are a baptized Catholic find a holy priest to hear your confession. Cleanse your soul, and begin anew! If you don't have a Bible of your own go out and buy one (as a Catholic, make sure you buy a Catholic version so you have access to all the books in the Bible the Catholic Church includes) and make a commitment to read from it every day. If this is new for you, begin with one of the Gospels and read a small section each day, ponder it, and ask the Holy Spirit to show you anything that you need to see. Don't rush. Pause and investigate passages, look up definitions of words, read notations on the page. Keep at it and keep reading, moving on to the Book of Acts and then through the books that follow. You will be amazed at how much you will learn and how applicable God's word is to our everyday life. Write little notes in your Bible, highlight things that stand out, date passages that are especially meaningful.

You are an educator. You spend your days teaching others how to study and develop their minds. Take that approach for yourself and become a student of God's Word and the Catholic Church. Read, research, attend conferences/talks, etc. There is nothing more valuable that you can do for your life!

Just a little word of caution! In the fervor of this journey we can become judgmental as we see things in God's Word and then notice how starkly opposed to this Word those around us are living. Don't fall into this trap. Take your journey humbly and work

---

3. John Paul II, *15th World Youth Day Address.*

on yourself. Spend your time listening to the Holy Spirit for areas that need to change and grow in you. Whatever you see in others, take it to prayer and let God deal with them. Resist the urge to fix everyone else and remember that this is about you and God—not you and everyone else!

Don't wait any longer—get going!

Personal Prayer and Study

SPEAKING OF THE GOVERNING institutions in the Church, Pope Benedict said, "The bureaucracy is spent and tired . . . It is sad that there are what you might call professional Catholics who make a living on their Catholicism, but in whom the spring of faith flows only faintly, in a few scattered drops."[1]

Fr. Raymond J. de Souza, in a commentary on Pope Benedict's words, states:

> It is easy enough to point to the managerial bishop or the administrative pastor and lament the lack of fervor for the faith and the absence of evangelical criteria in decision-making. But could not the same be said of any diocesan office, the staff room of any Catholic school, the executive officers of any Catholic social welfare agency or the bureaucrats that administer the vast panoply of Catholic organizations? Is it not the case that so many regard their position as membership in a club or as an officer of an enterprise, but not primarily as disciples or missionaries? The great sadness of which the Holy Father speaks is that over several generations now so many lay Catholics—"professional Catholics"—are marked by a deep-adopted clericalism themselves, comporting themselves as members of a privileged caste.[2]

So here we face a very critical question. As Catholic educators, where do we stand? Could we possibly be functioning in that

1. Benedict, *Deus Caritas Est.*
2. De Souza, *Why Are So Many.*

mindset of a "professional Catholic"—someone working within and for the Church without really understanding the incredible responsibility and privilege that it is? It happens very easily, and I can say without hesitation that I fit into this category in the first Catholic school I taught in early on in my professional career. I wasn't there because I knew God called me to Catholic education and I wasn't there because I understood how important it was that faith be the foundation of education. Had I not been pink-slipped due to a millage defeat in the public school district I was teaching in, I probably would never have ended up in that Catholic school. This school was a prominent Catholic school in the community. I considered myself a "good person" and a good teacher, but I truly was someone who did not understand the great responsibility and privilege I had before me as a Catholic educator. Though I attended Mass every Sunday, my faith really didn't extend much beyond that. My prayer life was minimal and purposeful study of the faith was close to nonexistent. I wasn't reading Scripture or anything else to develop my spiritual life. I didn't know Christian music existed and didn't realize that what I was listening to was doing nothing to encourage my spirit—wearing away at it many times instead. So, please understand, I know what it means to "not have a clue" about what I had entered into. Now, at this point in my life, I look back saddened, knowing that my students deserved better and that Christ desired so much more for me and my students. I let them and myself down, but more importantly I let God down.

Administrators—where are you in this picture? Do you realize the great responsibility you hold as you take the reigns of a school and make critical decisions regarding staffing, curriculum, programs, and everything else that falls under your mantle of authority? Though I respected the principal of that Catholic school and knew he was skilled in administration, I can also say without a doubt that academics outranked faith development. Of course, every classroom had religion as a subject but it was the "fit it in when you can" subject. I was never asked how I was teaching it or how it was impacting my students, or even how often I was teaching it. To be very transparent, I was not at all equipped to teach it!

It was not a topic of discussion at staff meetings, nor was it a class that was observed and evaluated. And to be very honest, my faith life was not even a part of the conversation in my interview. As administrators, how important is it to you that the teachers that you hire have a vibrant faith life? Do you consider that essential to their hiring or do you possibly look the other way if you find yourself in a pinch for a teacher or are facing a choice between someone dynamic in their academic discipline but lukewarm in faith, versus someone less dynamic instructionally but solid spiritually? What holds more long-term value for you? If you can't have a combination of the two, which would you choose?

I ask these questions because they are essential to our discussion regarding our personal prayer and study—especially since our personal prayer and study directly impacts those we serve in our Catholic schools.

> Do you not realize that, though all the runners in the stadium take part in the race, only one of them gets the prize? Run like that—to win. Every athlete concentrates completely on training, and this is to win a wreath that will wither, whereas ours will never wither. So that is how I run, not without a clear goal; and how I box, not wasting blows on air. I punish my body and bring it under control to avoid any risk that, having acted as herald for others, I myself may be disqualified.
>
> —1 Corinthians 9:24–30 (NJB)

Do you have a clear (spiritual) goal for our own life and are you wholeheartedly pursuing it? Are you willing to exert great effort and overcome possible laziness and self-centeredness to pursue Christ and knowledge of our Catholic faith? If not, how can you effectively help anyone else understand the goal, how can you help them win the prize? If not, then why are you really in Catholic education?

We must understand that there is no time for breaks and pauses in our faith life. Christian evangelist Greg Laurie puts it this way:

> Backsliding is not just falling backward, but it is also failing to go forward spiritually. If we are not moving

forward in Christ, then we are naturally going backward. In the Christian life, there is no standing still. We are either progressing or regressing. You show me a person who is failing to move forward spiritually, and by that I mean a person who is growing as a follower of Jesus, who is deepening in his or her prayer life and study of Scripture and likeness to Jesus, and I will show you a person who has begun the process of backsliding.[3]

This is serious business! Luke 17: 1–3 (NJB) states:

He said to His disciples, "Causes of falling are sure to come, but alas for the one through whom they occur! It would be better for such a person to be thrown into the sea with a millstone round the neck than to be the downfall of a single one of these little ones. Keep watch on yourselves!"

God takes the impartation of His truth to children very seriously, and if you are one who holds responsibility for the transmission of faith in education God is saying very clearly, "Keep watch on yourselves!"

So . . . are you keeping watch on yourself, are you running the race to win the prize, or are you boxing at the air with no aim, no goal, no understanding to pass along? I wonder if Jesus were to sit in on interviews for teachers and administrators, if He were to sit in on our faculty meetings (or our faculty lounges during breaks), or sit in on our conversations with parents—would He be in agreement with our priorities, our emphasis, our approach? What would He tell parents they should be looking for in a Catholic school?

All of these thoughts and questions point right back into the direction of where we are personally. It has to start there. You can't give what you don't have! Our culture and our schools are in crisis and extreme measures are needed! We can't say we don't have time or we are too busy. Our prayer and study has to be a priority. Oftentimes I will hear pastors say "If you only can spend five minutes each day, then spend five minutes." I DISAGREE! I guess if you

3. Laurie, "What Every Believer Should Know."

do nothing, five minutes is better than nothing, but what you do is too important to spend ONLY five minutes a day. Your prayer and study is the foundation for your ministry with God's precious children. You have to be prepared, equipped, and filled to the brim yourself so that it flows naturally in your words, your actions, your decisions, your discipline, and your planning.

Let's use the example of someone who needs dialysis. It is time-consuming, inconvenient, uncomfortable, etc., but without it death would be the result. It is the same with God. Not spending the time with Him in prayer and study of His Word and His Church—no matter how inconvenient or uncomfortable at first—would be a choice for the decline of your spiritual health. And if you are not healthy spiritually you cannot provide a spiritually healthy environment for others. Would you seek advice about health from someone who is clearly unhealthy? NO—you would want to talk to and model someone whose life reflects that effort.

Take a moment to consider all the things you do and plan in a day that you consider essential. You plan your meals, you plan your day's activities, you plan entertainment, what shows you will watch on television, you plan playing a game of basketball with friends, golfing, etc., you may plan an exercise routine, a weekly gathering with friends, a shopping trip, an outing. Consider the time and effort you might put into planning a vacation, browsing through Facebook, tweeting, twittering, Snapchatting or checking emails. The list could go on and on. According to research released in January 2013 by Ipsos Open Thinking Exchange, the average American spends more than three hours a day on social media. In March of 2014 the *New York Daily News* reported research that the average American spends five hours a day watching TV. That's more than eight hours a day! That's a full work day![4] Now add in all the other things you choose to do with your time, and no wonder we are spiritually starving. Do we as Americans seriously think all this time spent is really contributing anything of value to our lives?

Now stop for a minute and honestly evaluate the planning of your prayer and study time. How much time and effort do you

4. Marketing Charts, "Social Networking."

devote to God, His Word, and His Church? As you carry the responsibility that comes with being a Catholic educator, how prepared are you to do that effectively? Again, you can't give what you don't have! To be an effective Catholic/Christian educator you have to be tenacious about your faith. You have to be willing to give it the priority it deserves and requires.

We and our children are bombarded daily in this culture with immorality, violence, selfishness, relativism, and addictions. Daily we need our spiritual nourishment and guidance to have the wisdom and strength to stand in the face of all that opposes God with courage and fortitude. We need to actively develop virtue in our hearts, a strong sense of right and wrong, and a clear understanding of our faith to be able to journey through and address those very challenging issues of our day.

In God's wisdom He doesn't give us the whole picture and then send us out to accomplish His will. He knows we need Him every day and so He gives us a little bit at a time, enough for the next step. When you string together the "next steps" the plan unfolds as He intends. Psalm 119:105 (NRSV) says: "Your word is a lamp to my feet and a light on my path." In an article written by Gary Byers for the Association for Biblical Research he compares this Scripture to the actual use of ancient lamps:

> While ancient lamps were not designed for travel, they would illumine our way at night. Admittedly one wouldn't be going far, but the average one-wicker lamp would have been sufficient light to carefully move about the family compound. So Psalm 119:105 offers confidence that God's word would illumine my way like one of those lamps. Not unlike how I've used my cell phone to get around in the dark, they would have basically provided just enough light to illumine one step at a time.[5]

If God has designed His word to be a "lamp" unto our feet we are meant to seek it for our daily steps as individuals and educators.

No matter how faithful we think we may be in regards to this, there is always room to grow and improve. I spent many years in

5. Byers, "Lesson of the Lamp."

the haphazard manner of prayer. Thankfully, over the years I grew to realize its daily importance and significance, but I still have room for growth. The more I learn and experience, the more I realize how much more there is to learn! In writing this chapter I was so taken aback by the social media and TV statistics that I had to pause and evaluate my own habits. I don't have a Facebook account or spend much time on social media, but my TV viewing habits certainly have room for improvement, and I certainly check my phone for texts and emails much too frequently. I began to think of the time spent after dinner from 6–8 p.m., when our TV is on, wasting our time with the news, Jeopardy, Wheel of Fortune or other unnecessary, mindless viewing. How much more valuable would it be to my life and my family if I spent that time reading, studying, or watching things that would help develop and inform me in my faith? As I write these words I'm convicted again and plan to make some changes! I hope you will too.

There are no set rules to follow. Just begin! Consider something you can do without in your day and use that time instead to spend time with God! Find a quiet place in your home that can be "your spot." Talk to God, thank Him as you recount the blessings in your day, ask Him for guidance in areas where you have concerns personally and for others. Pick up a Bible and begin somewhere and read a little every day. Choose one with commentaries on each page to help you understand what is being taught. Have a dictionary close by to look up words that stand out to you, maybe even a notebook to jot down thoughts that cross your mind. Choose one good book about your Catholic faith and read a little every day. You will be amazed at how your life will begin to transform and your mind will be enlightened.

Don't wait any longer—begin NOW! Your spiritual health and life depends upon it—and so does the spiritual life and health of those you serve. And please remember that God always provides people to help us on our journey if we are sincerely seeking Him. I remember feeling like I had no idea where to begin to establish a consistent prayer life, but there were people around me that I knew had one. It just takes a little humility to be able to say that you could use some help and then a willingness to take the first step and commit to sticking with your plan day in and day out!

> Let the risen Jesus enter your life—welcome Him as a friend, with trust; He is life! If up till now you have kept Him at a distance, step forward. He will receive you with open arms. If you have been indifferent, take a risk; you won't be disappointed. If following Him seems difficult, don't be afraid. Trust Him, be confident that He is close to you, He is with you, and He will give you the peace you are looking for and the strength to live as He would have you do.[6]

6. Francis, *Joy of Discipleship*, 33.

The Ministry to Educate

IT'S NOT A JOB—IT'S a calling!

Each person reading this may, and probably does, have a different reason they became a teacher. Perhaps it was a dream you had as a little girl or boy, maybe it is because of a teacher that inspired you along the way, or because you love to learn and want to pass that along. Or maybe you didn't know what else to do and became a teacher because you liked the idea of a flexible schedule when you have children of your own. You may have received great teacher training, as I felt I did, but I would venture to guess that even if you attended a Catholic or Christian college your preparation to become an authentic, vibrant, Spirit-filled educator was sorely lacking. Though I know there are a few colleges and universities that take this seriously, the very frank truth is that most institutions do not challenge you in your faith and do not prepare you to become authentic Catholic Christian educators as they prepare you to provide academic instruction. The reasons can be countless, but the reason to become a Catholic educator is very direct and very simple.

The word "education" comes from the Latin word *educare* or *educere*, which means "to draw out that which lies within." Of course, as we educate we want to draw out the gifts and talents of each child—but from a Catholic Christian faith perspective it means so much more! "To draw out that which lies within" means to draw out the most important thing that lies within each of us—and that is the Spirit of God. As a Catholic educator you are being called to draw out of yourself, the students you serve, and those you work and interact with the very best within them, which is Christ! Ponder that for a moment and then consider how off-balance and out of perspective our present-day education system is—outside of and, yes, inside the Church. We are trained at a very literal level that education is the acquisition of knowledge, facts, skills, benchmarks, etc. It saddens me to see all the time that is wasted circling around trends, research, and the latest and greatest advancements in technology and learning. I am not saying that it is all useless, but I am saying that it is out of order—especially for Catholic schools. I have served on many committees and boards and over and over I have heard essentially the same things as people labored over how to increase enrollment, outshine the competition, achieve the best reputation. In one meeting I even heard, "Let's research what the public likes about the local public schools and let's advertise how we do it better." How sad and how alarmingly true was that statement, because basically that is what many schools are doing—trying to outdo, out-enroll, outsmart all the other schools. Money is raised and spent on more beautiful facilities, catchier advertising, more profound mission statements, better athletic teams, and everyone just keeps circling around the same wagon—though trying desperately to look like that is not the case.

Since my return to the Catholic Church and Catholic education I have had the opportunity to serve on committees that were established specifically for the strengthening of the Catholic identity of diocesan schools. During that time—on my own and along with others I have read through thousands of pages of Church documents and articles on Catholic education. I have binders filled with articles I have printed and referenced. I've read and reread, highlighted, tabbed, and tried to share so much of what I read. The more I read, the more my love for the Church's mission to educate our young grew and the more passionate I became. And the more I read, the more I sadly wondered why we have wandered so far from the beautiful truth and encouragement of our Church. I think about the millions of children who have not gotten the best of what God and the Church desires to give them. At this point it doesn't help to continue discussing how and why we got to this point. Though it's helpful to know and understand those things, there comes a point when it's just time to put it behind us and start anew! In the words of Blessed Mother Teresa, "Yesterday is gone; tomorrow has not yet come. We have only today. Let us begin."[1]

Though I wish I could, I can't possibly share in this little book all the statements, quotes, and words of truth from Church documents on education that inspired, challenged, and propelled me with urgency as an educator. What I will do, though, is highlight a lecture by Archbishop J. Michael Miller C. S. B. (Secretary for the Vatican's Congregation for Catholic Education), "The Holy See's Teaching on Catholic Schools," posted October 1, 2005. In this lecture Archbishop Miller references what he calls the five non-negotiables of Catholic identity—the lofty ideals proposed by the Holy See which inspire the Church's enormous investment in schooling. Most of what I share will be direct words from this lecture but will only be highlights of this lecture. I would certainly encourage pulling up the document to read it in its entirety. Information on how to access it can be found in the bibliography.

1. Inspired by a Supernatural Vision

> The enduring foundation on which the Church builds her educational philosophy is the conviction that it is a process which forms the whole child, especially with his or her eyes fixed on the vision of God. The specific purpose of a Catholic education is the formation of boys and girls who will be good citizens of this world, enriching society with the leaven of the gospel, but who will also be citizens of the world to come. Catholic schools have a straightforward goal: to foster the growth of good Catholic human beings who love God and neighbor and thus fulfill their destiny of becoming saints.

1. Teresa, *In The Heart of the World*, 17.

If we fail to keep in mind this high supernatural vision, all our talk about Catholic schools will be no more than what 1 Corinthians 13:1 describes as a gong booming or a cymbal clashing.

Question to Ponder

If we are called as educators to help students become saints, how can we possibly achieve that if "becoming saints" is not our own personal mission?

2. Founded on Christian Anthropology

> Emphasis on the supernatural destiny of students, on their holiness, brings with it a profound appreciation of the need to perfect children in all their dimensions as images of God. As we know, grace builds on nature. Because of this complementarity of the natural and the supernatural, it is especially important that all those involved in Catholic education have a sound understanding of the human person. Especially those who establish, teach in, and direct a Catholic school must draw on sound anthropology that addresses the requirements of both natural and supernatural perfection . . .

> Christ is not an afterthought or add-on to Catholic educational philosophy, but the center and fulcrum of the entire enterprise, the light enlivening every pupil who comes into our schools . . .

> The gospel of Christ and His very person are, therefore, to inspire and guide the Catholic school in its every dimension; its philosophy of education, its curriculum, community life, its selection of teachers, and even its physical environment. As Pope John Paul II wrote in his 1979 message to the National Catholic Association of the United States: "Catholic education is above all a question of communicating Christ, of helping to form Christ in the lives of others."

Question to Ponder

If you attended a Catholic or Christian college was this focus a foundational part of your teacher education? Applause if it was, but I would dare to say that for most, nothing like this was ever taught. Why is it that so many of our Catholic colleges aren't intentional about spiritually preparing graduates to effectively and faithfully teach in Catholic schools? Perhaps you would say it is because most graduates intend to teach in public schools. And why is that? Is it the money? And . . . if this was a foundational part of the training of teachers in Catholic colleges, how much more would these teachers have to offer in a public-school setting if that is sincerely where they felt the Lord wanted them?

3. Animated by Communion and Community

The Declaration *Gravissimum Educationis* notes an important advance in the way a Catholic school is thought of: the transition from the school as an institution to the school as a community. Even more Vatican statements emphasize that the school is a community of persons and, even more to the point, "a genuine community of faith" . . .

Elementary schools should try to create a community school climate that reproduces, as far as possible, the warm and intimate atmosphere of family life. Those responsible for these schools will, therefore, do everything they can to promote a common spirit of trust and spontaneity . . .

During childhood and adolescence a student needs to experience personal relations with outstanding educators, and what is taught has greater influence on the student's formation when placed in a context of personal involvement, genuine reciprocity, coherence of attitudes, lifestyle and day-to-day behavior . . .

What is human and visible can bear the divine. If Catholic schools are to be true to their identity, they should try to suffuse their environment with this delight in the sacramental. Therefore, they should express physically and visibly the external signs of Catholic culture through images, signs, symbols, icons, and other objects of traditional devotion; a chapel, classroom crucifixes and statues, signage, celebrations, and other sacramental reminders of good Catholic ecclesial life.

Question to Ponder

When you and others walk into your school and classroom, is your and others' spirit touched and inspired by the atmosphere? Is your school and classroom a place that celebrates the beauty of the Catholic faith? Does it feel like a family consisting of educators who live outside of school what they profess inside school? A Catholic school should be an oasis of faith, hope, and love. It should be a place that would never compromise its identity for anything—even public funds that "will help the students." Where does your school and your classroom fall, where could there be improvement and growth?

4. Imbued with a Catholic Worldview

A fourth distinctive characteristic of Catholic schools which always finds a place in the Holy See's teaching is this. Catholicism should permeate not just the class period of catechism or religious education, or the school's pastoral activities, but the entire curriculum. The Vatican documents speak of "an integral education, an education which responds to all the needs of the human person." This is why the Church establishes schools: because they are a privileged place which fosters the formation of the whole person. An integral education aims to develop gradually every capability of every student: their intellectual, physical, psychological, moral, and religious dimensions. It is "intentionally directed to the growth of the whole person" . . .

Catholicism has a particular "take" on reality that should animate its schools. It is a "comprehensive way of life" to be enshrined in the school's curriculum. One would comb in vain Vatican documents on schools to find anything about lesson planning, the order of teaching the various subjects, or the relative merit of different didactic methodologies. On the other hand, the Holy See does provide certain principles and guidelines which inspire the content of the curriculum if it is to deliver on its promise of offering students an integral education. Let's look at two of these: the principle of truth and the integration of faith, culture and life.

4.1 Search for Wisdom and Truth

In an age of information overload, Catholic schools must be especially attentive to the delicate balance between human experience and understanding. In the words of T. S. Eliot, we do not want our students to say: "We had the experience but missed the meaning" . . .

Catholic schools take up the daunting task of freeing boys and girls from the insidious consequences of what Benedict XVI recently called the "dictatorship of relativism"— a dictatorship which cripples all genuine education. Catholic educators are to have in themselves and develop in others a passion for truth which defeats moral and cultural relativism. They are to educate "in the truth."

4.2 Faith, Culture and Life

A second principle governing all Catholic education from the apostolic age down to the present is the notion that the faithful should be engaged in transforming culture in light of the gospel. Schools prepare students to relate the Catholic faith to their particular culture and to live that faith in practice . . .

A primary, but hardly only, way of guiding students to becoming committed Catholics, as we have discussed in emphasizing the importance of an integrated curriculum, is providing solid religious instruction. To be sure, "education in the faith is a part of the finality of a Catholic school." For young Catholics, such instruction embraces both knowledge of the faith and fostering its practice. Still, we must always take special care to avoid thinking that a Catholic school's distinctiveness rests solely on the shoulders of its religious education program. Such a position fosters the misunderstanding that faith and life are divorced, that religion is a merely private affair with neither a specific content nor moral obligations.

Question to ponder

How hard are educators working to find and create a curriculum that supports and teaches truth side-by-side with academic content? As standard curriculum becomes more and more distorted and absent of truth, are teachers able to detect the distortions and teach their students what those distortions are, or are we just going on day by day, teaching from the text with no clear understanding of where the errors are? Why are there so few Catholic publishers of curriculum? How did we allow the publishing of curriculum for our schools to be left to secular publishers? Are you willing to consider quality "Christian" curricula if Catholic materials are not available?

5. Sustained by the Witness of Teaching

In a word, those involved in Catholic schools, with very few exceptions, should be practicing Catholics committed to the Church and living her sacramental life. Despite the difficulties involved—which you know all too well—it is, I believe, a serious mistake to be anything other than "rigorists" about the personnel hired. The Catholic school system in Ontario, Canada, where I was raised, when pressured by public authorities for what they regarded as reasonable accommodations, relaxed this requirement for a time. The result was disastrous. With the influx of non-Catholic teachers, many schools ended up by seriously compromising their Catholic identity. Children absorbed, even if they were not taught, a soft indifferentism which sustained neither their practice of the faith nor their ability to imbue society with authentically Christian values. Principals, pastors, trustees, and parents share, therefore, in the serious duty of hiring teachers who meet the standards of doctrine and integrity of life essential to maintaining and advancing a school's Catholic identity . . .

We need teachers with a clear and precise understanding of the specific nature and role of Catholic education. The careful hiring of men and women who enthusiastically endorse a Catholic ethos is, I would maintain, the primary way to foster a school's catholicity. The reason for such concern about teachers is straightforward. Catholic education is strengthened by its "martyrs." Like the early church, it is built up through the shedding of their blood. Those of us who are, or have been, teachers know all about that. But I am speaking here about "martyrs" in the original sense of "witnesses" . . .

As well as fostering a Catholic view across and throughout the curriculum, even in so-called secular subjects, "if students in Catholic schools are to gain a genuine experience of the Church, the example of teachers and others responsible for their formation is crucial: the witness of adults in the school community is a vital part of the school's identity." Children will pick up far more by example than by masterful pedagogical techniques, especially in the practice of Christian virtues . . .

Educators at every level in the Church are expected to be models for their students by bearing transparent witness to the gospel. If boys and girls are to experience the splendor of the Church, the Christian example of teachers and others responsible for their formation is crucial . . .

The prophetic words of Pope Paul VI ring as true today as they did thirty years ago: "Modern man listens more willingly to witnesses than to teachers, and if he does listen to teachers, it is because they are witnesses." What teachers do and how they act are more significant than what they say—inside and outside the classroom. That's how the Church evangelizes. "The more completely an educator can give concrete witness to the model of the ideal person [Christ] that is being presented to the students, the more this ideal will be believed and imitated." Hypocrisy particularly turns off today's students. While their demands are high, perhaps sometimes even unreasonably so, there is no avoiding the fact that if teachers fail to model fidelity to the truth and virtuous behavior, then even the best of curricula cannot successfully embody a Catholic school's distinctive ethos.

Question to Ponder

I have no comment. I believe the above says it all!

Professional Prayer Life

IT MAY SEEM STRANGE to see a chapter titled "Professional Prayer Life," but I believe it is essential that every Catholic/Christian educational institution foster the professional prayer lives of its faculty and staff. I will say, however, that a genuine professional prayer life is not possible without first having a genuine "personal prayer life."

But for the sake of this topic, let's assume we are talking about a faculty and staff who do understand the importance of a personal prayer life. Everyone may not be at the same spot—some may be more seasoned, some may just be starting out, and some in between, but there is no argument that a personal prayer life is essential. With that understanding clear, it is critical that the faculty and staff of a Catholic school have a clear commitment to praying together. I would go so far as to say that it is more important than professional development meetings, PLCs, etc. Now, I am not saying professional development is not important. Clearly it is. But praying together should be first on the list before anything else. It stabilizes our perspective and helps us keep priorities right. It can provide direction and guidance regarding our path. Then, when we work together on professional development, we are doing it with the guidance and support of the Holy Spirit. We don't do things just for the sake of doing them; we choose carefully and wisely.

Praying together as professionals encourages community, care, and understanding for one another. No matter how spiritual a school is there will always be tensions, disagreements, misunderstandings, jealousies, hurts, and disappointments. Schools—just

like the Church—are made up of imperfect, vulnerable human beings. It is through a shared prayer life that we learn to understand
one another, learn to forgive one another, and learn to die to self
for the welfare of a greater good.

Praying together as professionals sets the stage—it shows children, parents, extended church family that this is critical to our wellbeing. It is a sign of humility and a sign that we recognize our need
to depend upon God rather than ourselves. Joint prayer reminds us
that we do not and cannot have all the answers. It reflects that we realize our perspective and vision is limited and that only God sees the
whole picture and only He can provide divine wisdom. Joint prayer
helps us establish a pattern of response to every need, every concern,
and every plan. It is our beginning and our end.

How do we set the course for this type of prayer? Well, as
I implied earlier, we cannot do something with others that we
haven't first done for ourselves. To pray as a group without being
committed to personal prayer is like coming to a meeting without
having first read the documents that will be discussed at the meeting. You may be present but you will not be adequately prepared.
But let's assume the need for personal prayer is understood; how
do you establish a good routine of professional prayer in a school?

First of all, I would say that prayer as a professional team
should happen every day! It should hold such a place of importance in our ministry that the day cannot begin without it. Schedules should be created that require staff to arrive early enough to
be able to gather together for prayer before the day begins. You
don't have to get stressed over creating something; use something
solid that is already prepared. There are wonderful resources available—the Magnificat, The Word Among Us daily reflections, etc.
Choose something together and use it diligently—every day! The
topics or content won't be the primary issue, because people of
prayer understand that God will miraculously meet them where
they are. One of my favorite resources is The Word Among Us daily
reflections. Each week I would print off the daily posts for the next
week and I would have them copied and organized and stacked by
day in the staff lounge. That way no one had to be "the leader" of

prayer. The sheets were prepared and ready so if anything unexpected came up for anyone, things were always ready and anyone could get things going. I also really liked these reflections because it always had a reference for Scripture to be read, with a reflection applying to what was said. Over and over the reflection for the day would hit right on the target of something we were struggling with relationally, professionally, or spiritually. The reflections set our course for the day, kept us humble by reminding us of our sinful nature, and strengthened us in hope for difficulties we were facing. Many times teachers would take the reflection and share it with their students that day because it applied to something they were dealing with in their classrooms or to some struggle they knew a particular student was having. If we just give God the chance to speak to us He will address so much of what we face in our schools. He wants to speak to our needs, but unfortunately too often we leave Him out and try to rationalize and strategize on our own. Every school day that starts with prayer should end with prayer. If the community is small enough, perhaps everyone could physically gather together and pray to end the day before being dismissed. If that's not realistic, perhaps prayer over the intercom could work. Essentially, though, as much as we all need prayer to begin our school day, we also need it to end our school day, to equip and strengthen each individual for what they are heading home to tackle.

I also believe there should be opportunities for times to prepare a retreat for extended reflection and prayer. I think each school should have a beginning-of-the-year, middle-of-the-year, and end-of-the-year day of reflection and prayer. Setting aside a full day or two to spiritually reset and recharge is crucial for a school community. Educating our young is a huge task, and it brings stresses and challenges that most people who are not educators do not understand. Time set aside is needed to spiritually prepare for a new school year, spiritually recharge in the middle, and come together with thanksgiving at the end.

Another aspect of prayer together as a community is the Mass. I grew up attending a small Ukrainian Catholic elementary school and every day began with Mass! Nothing began academically until we first had Mass as a school community, then we all went to our classrooms to begin our academic instruction. I still remember the warmth and comfort I felt as a small child sitting in that church each morning. I know that the daily reception of the Eucharist strengthened my heart and prepared it for my journey of faith that lie ahead. I know that I felt we were all one community under our banner of faith and that we were in this daily task of school together. It felt like family—and it was: it was the family of God every day, giving Him our firstfruits of the day. I remember as a small child looking around at all the beautiful icons and thinking about Mary and all the saints. I felt their presence with us. I was proud of that, I was comforted by that, and I was strengthened by that. I have never forgotten those days! Now think about it, I am talking about the 1960s—a time when families were stronger, faith was more a part of everyday life, our government was not actively trying to minimize our Christian faith, a time when we could never have imagined days such as the ones we face today. If I was strengthened during those times, how much more do the children we teach today need that! Faith is under attack, families are under attack (many broken forever), religious freedom is under attack, Mass attendance is in decline, young people are exiting the faith in record numbers, and the list goes on and on. How do we stop the bleeding? Maybe, just maybe, our Catholic schools can make a difference by becoming places of genuine prayer. I believe that getting our priorities straight and giving God the beginning and end of our days will open us up to new blessings, new insights, and new possibilities. And don't keep it to yourself—invite your parents to participate!

Pray, pray, pray. In addition to those times set aside to pray, pray spontaneously throughout the day with students. Pray before tests, during conflicts, if someone is sick, before lunch. Pray when there is good news, pray when there is sad news. Pray for one another's families, pray for our country, our government leaders, our Church, our pastors, for the things we hope for and for the things we fear. Help children see that prayer should take place all day for all kinds of things—that any and every need should receive prayer followed with thanksgiving for God's attention to our prayers. When we do this we truly live the Scripture: "Rejoice at all times. Pray without ceasing. Give thanks in all circumstances, for this is God's will for you in Christ Jesus" (1 Thess 5:16–18, NRSV).

How sad it must be to God to hear school communities say, "We just don't have the time, we have academic time requirements we need to meet." Seriously? I would say if we don't have time for God to be the center of everything, then we might as well become a charter school. Giving God first place should only increase our productivity and effectiveness. We can't be mediocre when Christ is at the center. We can't waste our time because He calls for excellence, and if we seek Him dilligently He will help us be excellent! I would urge diocesan leaders who oversee Catholic schools to consider if the spiritual, emotional, and educational wellbeing of children will come more from following rigid state and local guidelines that tie your hands and keep you from implementing something like daily Mass, or from a rich, prayer-filled school environment that is laser-focused on the spiritual development of the child followed by rich, disciplined academic instruction.

Principals, when you are seeking individuals for positions within your school, ask them about their prayer life and pay attention. Do they get excited to talk about it? Do they have stories of answered prayers and evidence of God's presence? Do they express a desire to have that be a central part of their position within your school? You will learn a lot about a candidate when you ask them to tell you about their prayer life.

The times are desperate and call for a radical reorganization of our schools! I am writing this in the midst of the 2016 presidential election process. Each day as I turn on the news I am reminded of the desperate state of our country and culture. If not now, when, and if not us, who?

Practices That Enhance

WE HAVE TALKED ABOUT the importance of a personal relationship with Christ, the importance of personal prayer, the importance of professional prayer, and have touched on the idea of daily Mass. Now I'd like to expound a bit on the importance of Mass and on other Catholic practices that enhance and strengthen our faith lives.

Daily Mass

Catechism of the Catholic Church #1324 states that "The Eucharist is the source and summit of Christian life."[1]

A simple definition of "source"—something that provides what is needed. A simple definition of "summit"—the highest level that can be reached. Now if our Catechism says that the Eucharist is what we need and is the highest we can go, then why wouldn't celebrating Mass together as many times a week as is possible be our priority? How can it be that some schools do only once a week, once a month, or maybe once a quarter? Would we ever approach food for our body that way? Of course not! Then why do we approach our spiritual food that way? Shouldn't we be teaching our children that they should take advantage of participating in the Mass and receiving the Eucharist as often as possible? Do we think they will figure it out all on their own someday? Many of these children come from families that don't even attend Mass on Sundays! We have the privilege of helping them realize this while they

1. *Catechism of the Catholic Church*, #1324.

are under our care at school. How in good conscience could we ever let this take a back seat?

Mass doesn't have to be an hour long, but could easily be done within thirty minutes. If we plan well and have a pastor who takes this seriously there is no reason not to do it. At the all-girls Catholic high school where I served as principal we purposely placed Mass right before lunch. That was for two reasons. First, parents couldn't bring their daughters to school late "because they really don't want to go to Mass, and shouldn't be forced to go." To which I would say, then why do you have them in a Catholic school? Comments like that tell a lot about a person's perspective. So I avoided the Mass-before-classes-start arrangement. I felt compelled to place it right in the middle of the day before lunch, explaining that just as our chapel was at the center of our building, the Mass would be the center of our day. It gave us all the opportunity to come together midday to leave behind any stresses from the morning and be refreshed and spiritually fed. When asked what was one of their favorite things about our school, so many of these teenage girls would say, "We get to go to Mass every day!" Isn't that awesome? How often do you hear that? That comes from something being built into their day that they didn't know they needed so desperately but can clearly after time see the benefit of.

Confession

Catechism of the Catholic Church #1455—"The confession (or disclosure) of sins, even from a simply human point of view, frees us and facilitates our reconciliation with others. Through such an admission man looks squarely at the sins he is guilty of, takes responsibility for them, and thereby opens himself again to God and to the communion of the Church in order to make a new future possible."[2]

Confession should be made available on a regular basis to students and staff. In the Catholic elementary school where I was principal, we recruited priests from throughout our town to enable

2. *Catechism of the Catholic Church*, #1455.

us to provide confession once a month. We would set up a secure spot in the school for confession to take place and each month more and more students would desire to go. You could always tell it was "confession" day because there was a definite difference in the atmosphere of the school. There was a peace, a joy, and a lightness of heart that you almost felt you could touch! It was beautiful to behold! In the high school where we held daily Mass we always asked the priest if he could stay to hear confession. It wasn't always necessarily available every day but pretty close—at least three times a week. The gift this was to our young women who took advantage of the opportunity was amazing. Never did they have to walk around allowing heaviness to grow in their hearts over a sin committed. They knew confession and God's grace and forgiveness was readily available. The effect of taking advantage of that was obvious on the young women. It was obvious in how they carried themselves, in how they treated others, and on the peace that rested upon them. Getting rid of these burdens and accepting God's forgiving grace frees us up to attend to so many other things. We are not weighed down and preoccupied, but instead set free and light of heart and spirit.

This beautiful Catholic practice needs to be revived and protected in our schools. So start where you're at and strive to make it better—make it happen, make it important, and make it special. Do all you can to make this beautiful gift of the Sacrament of Reconciliation available as often as possible!

Adoration

The need, the importance, and the necessity of this beautiful practice of Eucharistic Adoration is evident in the words and directives of our most recent beloved popes.

> Anyone who has a special devotion to the sacred Eucharist and who tries to repay Christ's infinite love for us with an eager and unselfish love of his own will experience and fully understand—and this will bring great delight and benefit to his soul—just how precious is a

life hidden with Christ in God, and just how worthwhile it is to carry on a conversation with Christ, for there is nothing more consoling here on earth, nothing more efficacious for progress along the paths of holiness.
—Pope Paul VI, *Mysterium Fidei.*

I urge priests, religious and lay people to continue and redouble their efforts to teach the younger generations the meaning and value of Eucharistic Adoration and devotion. How will young people be able to know the Lord if they are not introduced to the mystery of His presence? Like the young Samuel, by learning the words of the prayer of the heart, they will be closer to the Lord, who will accompany them in their spiritual and human growth, and in the missionary witness which they must give throughout their life.
—Pope John Paul II, *Letter on the 75th Anniversary of the Feast of Corpus Christi #8.*

In a world where there is so much noise, so much bewilderment, there is a need for silent adoration of Jesus concealed in the Host. Be assiduous in the prayer of adoration and teach it to the faithful. It is a source of comfort and light, particularly to those who are suffering.
—Pope Benedict XVI, *Pastoral Visit of His Holiness Pope Benedict XVI in Poland: Address by the Holy Father.*

Moreover, I want to encourage everyone to visit—if possible, every day—especially amid life's difficulties, the Blessed Sacrament of the infinite love of Christ and His mercy, preserved in our churches, and often abandoned, to speak filially with Him, to listen to Him in silence, and to peacefully entrust yourself to Him.
—Pope Francis, "Message for Italy's Eucharistic Congress."

How much more clear can it be? As the noise, the confusion, and the activity of our lives continues to grow, how much more desperate does the need for this quiet time with Christ become? Each day we enter our schools knowing that we will encounter struggles. It is certain that each day there will be staff members as well as students who will be walking through our doors heavy of heart for some reason. Perhaps there is a struggle at home, perhaps a marriage is suffering or financial stress is present. Perhaps there is illness, fear, or personal insecurities of some sort. The list could go on and on exemplifying the certain truth from Scripture that "I have told you all this so that you may find peace in me. In the world you will have hardship, but be courageous I have conquered the world" (John 17:33, NJB). The hardship is certain and the answer to maintaining peace in the midst of the hardship is certain as well. It has been clearly laid out and spoken to us by our fathers in the faith—our popes. The need for this quiet time of reflection and prayer has always been important and needed, but never more than now. Never has our society been more Godless, never has the moral compass of our nation been more distorted and in need of transformation, but, as Pope Benedict so clearly said, it will not happen without Adoration. We must, as educators, heed the warning and the call. We must respond and make Adoration a priority in our schools! Whether you arrange for it to take place within the church building, a small chapel within your school, or a transformed classroom or space within your building, it can be done easily and it will surely transform the culture of your school. All you have to do is ask for God's help to put it all together and He will show up each and every time. He will soften hearts, change minds, build unity, grant peace, and transform lives. Your school community with be all the richer for making that commitment.

Begin by making a commitment to schedule Adoration into your school calendar for at least once a month. Make it a firm and unmovable part of your schedule. If you don't have easy access to a church building or a chapel within your school, create a sacred space once a month. It can be in a cafeteria, a gymnasium, a classroom, etc. If you don't have that, be creative and have the Blessed Sacrament travel to each of your classrooms on a particular day. Set that day as a "holy" day in your school. Teach the children to be quieter on that day, and silent when they pass the space being used for Adoration. Create an atmosphere of awe and reverence for the presence of the King of kings! You will be amazed at their willingness and the purity of their reverence.

In both Catholic schools where I served as principal formal Adoration took place once a month inside a chapel in our school building. Our academic schedule was altered and a schedule was set in both schools for time to be set aside for every classroom so that every child and staff member was assured of time before the Blessed Sacrament.

At the elementary level, the time in the chapel was organized to meet them where they were developmentally. I had two wonderful moms who created a very sweet time for each class, incorporating music, Scripture, group prayer, and some time for silence. In the five years I was at the school, I witnessed a beautiful transformation in the hearts of the children, culminating in my last year with an amazing Eucharistic Adoration experience (a miracle from my perspective). Our elementary children would have Eucharistic Adoration in the chapel, which was located in the middle school attached to our building. On February 4, 2011, we began our visits to the chapel for Adoration as we had so many times before, but this day was to be very different! Beginning with the first class that entered the chapel, an image of Jesus in the Blessed Sacrament was seen by the children and adults present. When one of the moms told me the children were seeing Jesus, I never thought they meant literally until I made my visit to the chapel and was overwhelmed with what I was seeing. It continued throughout the day, with a very defined glow resembling the Sacred Heart of Jesus growing in intensity. Word quickly spread into the community and many came to the school chapel to witness this. If you Google "Jackson, Michigan, Eucharistic Adoration miracle" you will find several articles on the event. The children witnessing this will never forget the experience. The following week I came to school with materials for every child to make a monstrance. I provided them with a round white paper circle and asked them to draw what they saw that day and to glue it on their monstrance. The clarity of their drawings. was amazing. One little kindergarten girl named Teja drew her picture of Jesus with tears coming down. When I asked why Jesus had tears, she said, "Oh, Mrs. Tarnacki, those aren't sad tears, those are tears of joy because Jesus was so happy to see us!"

How priceless is that! I will never know the extent of how all those Fridays in Adoration and in particular how that one day touched each heart, but I know for certain that it did. I know that as we gave priority to this time with God, He blessed each and every one of us in the way we most needed from Him.

At the high school level, we also held Adoration in our school chapel on the first Friday of each month. We altered our schedule and gave it the same priority. At this level the focus was on beautiful reflective music and designated times of silence. At this age the silence is so important, for where else in their lives will they find it? They are disconnected from all their technology and are given the opportunity to learn to sit quietly before the Lord. I found that initially this sitting quietly was difficult and felt very unnatural to some, but each time they came, they became more comfortable, and as a result the chapel on a daily basis became a more frequented place to just sit quietly and pray or reflect.

There are many resources to help plan this special time for children and young adults. If you understand the great need for this and ask God to help you put it all together, He will not let you down. He will help you create the schedule, guide you to appropriate materials, bring the people to help, and will fill whatever space you use with His presence and power.

Make sure to invite your parents on those days. It is a great gift to children to know that one or both of their parents see the value in setting aside time to come to school to pray before the Blessed Sacrament.

The Rosary

Catechism #2677 explains that "Because she gives us Jesus, her son, Mary is the Mother of God and our mother; we can entrust all our cares and petitions to her; she prays for us as she prayed for herself, 'Let it be to me according to your word.' By entrusting ourselves to her prayer, we abandon ourselves to her prayer, we abandon ourselves to the will of God together with her: 'Thy will be done.'"

As our heavenly mother we have access to Jesus through Mary. Why wouldn't we want to take advantage of this amazing gift and teach every child placed in our care about her love and mantle of protection for us? As a child I remember the rosary being a central part of our life. I still remember being maybe eight or nine and praying the rosary in my bed each night (for I don't know how long) so that my brother wouldn't be called up in the draft for the Vietnam War. As relatives all around us were being called, my brother never was! As a young child the innocent trust in prayers to Our Lady left an impression on me to this day.

There is a comfort in knowing we have a mother in heaven. That became very evident to me when I lost both parents within a year of each other at the age of twenty-two and twenty-three. I felt orphaned in a sense and found comfort in knowing she was there, though I had not continued my devotion to pray the rosary in my teenage years. Unfortunately, it was not a devotion regularly presented or practiced in my Catholic high school, and I lost my way in regards to this. Accessing the Blessed Mother was something I sadly let go of in the evangelical church we were so active in. One of my greatest joys when we returned to the Catholic faith (right behind the Eucharist) was a newfound love and appreciation for Mary and the beautiful prayer of the rosary.

As Catholic educators, we must keep this devotion for Mary and the rosary alive. Take a moment and research the fifteen promises made to St. Dominic by Mary, and you will be hard-pressed to come up with any excuse for not making sure this is a point of emphasis in your school community. Every child, no matter what age, will find great comfort and love in a sincere devotion to our Blessed Mother. Don't allow this to fall by the wayside.

There are many ways to incorporate opportunities to pray the Rosary. You can have opportunities available before school, after school, after Mass, a decade a day as part of morning prayer, etc. I remember as a child loving the month of May because of its significance in regards to Mary. Our annual May crowning left such an impact on me that I would do my own little May crownings for the statue of the Blessed Mother we had in the front of our home.

I can only imagine the smile on the faces of some of our neighbors as they saw me out there in the front yard once again creating my own imaginary procession and crowning the statue with a wreath of flowers. Let's restore that awe and wonder and return to Mary the honor she so rightly deserves.

The Examen

The Examen: an Ignatian practice that trains us to reflect on the events of our day discerning God's presence leading us to repentance, thanksgiving, and opportunities to make changes in our life.

Teaching our students to do this naturally each day could prepare them to continue a powerful practice that will benefit them spiritually the rest of their lives. It would be so easy for a school to use the five steps of the Examen to close out each day in prayer as a community.

1. Become aware of God's presence.

2. Review the day with gratitude.

3. Pay attention to your emotions.

4. Choose one feature of the day and pray from it.

5. Look toward tomorrow.

More detailed information can be found at IgnatianSpirituality.com.

Can you imagine the spirit of community that could be developed within each classroom and each school if every day the Examen was the model for end-of-the-day prayer? How much healing would occur in relationships if we all reflected on the day we just completed, acknowledging how God is present in our midst, thanking Him for His goodness to us that day, reflecting on how we are ending the day feeling (did something bring us joy, sadness, fear, etc.)—perhaps someone hurt our feelings or we hurt theirs? At this point each person could take a quiet moment to think about that, repent quietly, and then think about how they could make it right—an apology before leaving for the day, a short note to say they're sorry or a short note to let someone know how they blessed you that day. Each day we leave so many troubles unresolved and so many blessings unrecognized. What if we taught children to pay attention to these situations and act upon them? Could it transfer over to their lives at home, in their neighborhoods? Then, finally, closing with a short prayer asking God to guide us into our evenings and the next day with what we learned from the day. I can't imagine it not changing lives, not changing classroom settings, not changing school and parish communities, and not changing the homes of our students and staff.

The Examen: a short, easy-to-do style of prayer to practice at school, leaving a generation of children a little better equipped in this increasingly noisy culture to quiet their souls and make their world better.

Novenas

Every school community has times when special needs exist. There may be a student or staff member dealing with a serious illness or situation in their family, there could be physical, financial, or spiritual needs that exist within the school community. At these times that stand out from the ordinary we all need to learn to pray in a way that takes us out of the ordinary. That's where novenas come in. They are opportunities for a special emphasis of prayer for a certain length of time. They help us do something special together when we feel helpless.

In the words of Redemptorist Father Jim White, "Novenas aren't for controlling God, but for opening ourselves to God in order to increase our faith and grow in love of God and neighbor."[3]

In times of struggle or concern we need to be able to reach out with others for greater faith and trust that God has it all in control. I am writing these words fourteen days before the 2016 presidential election—an election filled with fear, uncertainty,

---

3. Fenelon, "Power of Novenas."

doubt, just about every negative emotion possible. What could I, aside from making sure to vote, do to try to make things better? The answer is prayer! As a nation a fifty-four day novena was encouraged by the Church. Praying that novena with my husband and the Church those fifty-four days brought me a sense of peace and trust. It helped me feel part of a bigger picture. It helped me feel like I was doing something important to help in the volatile atmosphere of this election. I have no idea how it will all turn out on November 8, but I know that many, many prayers were lifted up for God's help. Now He will answer in His wisdom and in His faithful ways.

Praying novenas together provides a wonderful opportunity to humble ourselves before God, present our needs together, and then watch Him work. There is no doubt that there would be times of miraculous answers. How awesome when those things occur to be able to rejoice together, knowing everyone played a part in praying for that answer to prayer!

Teaching children the beauty and power of praying novenas is another tool in their spiritual tool belt. As they grow and get older there will always be times of trouble that need a special emphasis of prayer. A novena is one of those special opportunities.

Scripture

As I discuss the importance of Scripture in our schools I know there could be some pushback. I have been pushed back at on this topic from well-meaning, faithful Catholics. To some, giving prominence to Scripture looks and feels too "Protestant." Many Catholics were not raised to read and reflect on Scripture. In our home there was a family Bible, but it was never opened as a family to read, discuss, and reflect upon. It sat on a coffee table looking nice but honestly of no use to anyone. That is just how things were and sadly still are for many. In thirteen years of Catholic education, Scripture was not something that was talked about EXCEPT with one teacher in my elementary school. Her name was Sr. John. She was my sixth- and seventh-grade teacher and was from the

Ukrainian order of the Sister Servants of Mary Immaculate. Sr. John was young and fun. She was always doing something out of the ordinary to catch our attention, spark our interest, and challenge us to give our best. I still recall many of the things she did, but one thing in particular that caught my attention was how she posted Scripture around the room. She would selectively choose verses to support her efforts to call us to higher ground. I remember distinctly times in the day when I would look around the room and read what she had put up. It spoke to my heart and stirred something in me. Though I was approaching my teenage years these verses left an impact I did not understand at the time. I still don't fully understand specific ways they guided me, but I know they caught my attention and provided something that I needed then or would need for the future. I was being drawn to God's Word and only wish as my education continued that there had been other teachers to to build upon what Sr. John sparked, but sadly there wasn't. Bible reading and Scripture study just was not and in many ways still is not a Catholic thing to do.

One of the supports I heard from a priest for not encouraging Bible reading at home was because the Catholic Church already provides a way for the faithful to hear God's word at Mass—in fact, the entire Bible is covered over three years, he said. I sat quietly for a moment because of my great respect for this priest, and then responded that, in my humble opinion, I felt that reasoning was sorely lacking in this day and age. For a person to "hear" the complete contents of the Bible over a three-year period, that person would have to attend Mass every day. How could we use this line of thinking in a time when weekly Sunday Mass has declined substantially and the numbers at daily Mass are very low. So if you don't go to daily Mass and frequently miss Sunday Mass, it's not taught in school, and you don't read it on your own, then how do you experience Scripture?

Holy Scripture is a lifeline! You can't read it and not be changed. The children in our schools need the hope and encouragement that God's Word brings. There has not been a challenge in my life I couldn't find Scripture to apply. It's never dated and it always applies.

In an article by Fr. Dwight Longenecker titled "Why Don't Catholics Read the Bible?," the following words encourage us to press forward to make Scripture a regular part of our lives as Catholics:

Take and Read

St. Augustine was converted when he heard children singing, "Tolle legge. Take and read! Take and read!" It was the Bible he picked up to read and the saving words of Scripture transformed his life and brought him to a true and constant conversion.

Our individual Catholic lives and the life of our Church would be infinitely improved if more of us took Bible reading seriously. We Catholics need more Bible scholars amongst our pastors. We need more homilies that are rooted in a profound understanding of Scripture. We need more resources for personal Bible reading. We need to understand the Scriptures better to see how our faith is rooted and grounded in the Bible. We need to hear the children singing, "Tolle legge. Take and read! Take and read!" . . .

Our own official teachings encourage us to read, study, and learn the Scriptures. *Dei Verbum*—a document about God's word from Second Vatican Council, says, "All clergy should remain in close contact with the Scriptures by means of reading and accurate study of the text . . . similarly the Council earnestly and expressly calls upon all the faithful . . . to acquire by frequent reading of holy Scripture the excellent knowledge of Jesus Christ (Philippians 3:8), for as St. Jerome said, 'Ignorance of the Scriptures is indeed ignorance of Christ.'"[4]

The Church clearly understood how important this is, but somehow we missed the mark when it came to communicating and guiding the faithful in this.

---

4. Longenecker, "Why Don't Catholics Read The Bible?"

Our Catholic schools have an amazing opportunity to help children develop a love for and a habit of reading Scripture. There is no reason for us not to include Scripture in our lessons, have Scripture posted in our halls and classrooms, use Scripture to encourage young hearts by having one we focus on each week as a classroom or school. Scripture can be used in little notes of encouragement to students, staff, parents, etc . . . Reading a little bit of Scripture together each morning can guide them to continue that practice long after they leave your school. Play games with it, help them get in the habit of committing Scripture to memory and turning to it in times of need. Teach them how Scripture changes and guides our hearts, instructs us in truth, and helps us understand God's love for us.

Protestants are criticized for relying too heavily on Scripture, but if we are honest Catholics could be criticized for relying on it too little. We have the best thing going as Catholics! If we could provide our students with a love for the Eucharist, a love for Church teaching, and a love for Scripture, how much better equipped would they be for the challenges of their personal, professional, and their spiritual lives!

So first fill your own hearts with God's word, and then let it overflow to the beautiful children in your care, the parents you serve, and the colleagues you spend each day with!

Holy Water

In an article from *The Catholic Exchange* titled "Hidden Power of Holy Water," by K. V. Turley, the following statement is made:

> In theological terms, holy water is a sacramental. It is a mixture of blessed salt and blessed water, and although, by its use, sanctifying grace is not conferred, actual grace is obtained. The *Catechism of the Catholic Church* teaches that sacramentals operate by means of the Church's intercession. We are told that, through the prayers of the Church, by the pious use of holy water, the intellect is enlightened, and the will moved from evil while being

prompted to do good; and both body and mind are thereby strengthened and healed.

In addition, ponder the following quotes:

From long experience I have learned that there is nothing like holy water to put devils to flight and prevent them from coming back again. They also flee from the Cross, but return; so holy water must have great virtue. For my own part, whenever I take it, my soul feels a particular and most notable consolation.[5]

—St. Teresa of Avila

I have myself felt an extraordinary consolation when I have used holy water. It is certain that I have felt a great joy and inner peace which I cannot describe, a joy with which my soul was quite refreshed. This is not merely an effect of the imagination, nor a rare occurrence. I have experienced it frequently and paid special attention to it. On these occasions I feel like one who, suffering intense thirst, takes a glass of water and is quite refreshed. From this we can see how important everything instituted by the Church is; it comforts me to see the great power which her blessing imparts to water, so great is the difference between blessed and unblessed water.[6]

—St. Teresa of Avila

From just these two small references to holy water you are stirred to consider why it is so infrequently used outside of church. These simple words prompted me to order a holy water font for our home! And as we discuss in this book the many things that impact the hearts and minds of the children in our Catholic schools you can't help but wonder why the use of holy water would not be a daily occurrence in our classrooms and school buildings. So many children (and adults) come to school each day carrying burdens we don't know of—they come with fears, anxieties, uncertainties,

---

5. Stanley, "The Power of Holy Water."
6. McKinney, "Effects of Holy Water."

and struggles. It would seem that careful teaching and easy access to holy water would be a blessing to everyone.

I have a great-niece—my nephew's daughter—Addison, who attends Spiritus Sanctus Academy in Ann Arbor, Michigan. This school is run by the Sisters of Mary Mother of the Eucharist. They are very intentional about the atmosphere of faith they create within their buildings and it touches the hearts of not only the children but the adults involved as well. I know that firsthand because my daughter taught there. But back to my great-niece—my nephew was raised Catholic but had not received the catechesis for a well informed, vibrant faith. His parents divorced when he was in second grade and he attended public school. Though my brother gave his best raising his three boys alone, that was one area where he felt ill-equipped. My nephew's wife converted to the Catholic faith early in their marriage, but she also did not receive rich instruction in her RCIA (Rite of Christian Initiation of Adults). Their choice to send their two children to Spiritus Sanctus came from a desire for them to have the support they needed to provide better faith formation than they had received themselves. Both children have learned so much and are thriving spiritually and academically in the school. My great-niece in particular displays such love for the Mass and for worship. She is presently in first grade. She loves to come home and plink away on her keyboard pretending she is leading worship. It is so beautiful to witness. Clearly she has learned as well the importance of holy water at school (where it is readily available and used often throughout the school day). Evidence of her clear understanding came recently when she was at her grandpa's house with her mom helping him prepare his house to be put up for sale. A showing was lined up for that evening and my nephew's wife texted me the time of the showing and asked me to pray it goes well. Below is our stream of texts:

Sarah—my nephew's wife:
8pm! Say a prayer everything falls into place with ease for him.

Me:
Just prayed! Maybe you and Addie and Mickey can say a little prayer together before they come. That would be awesome for Addie to witness—especially if these are the buyers!

Sarah:
She's ahead of you . . . she's been blessing his entire house with holy water for the past ½ hour, saying hopefully some nice people come and want to live in papa's nice house.

How amazing is that! As the adults prepare practically, the little six-year-old takes it upon herself to prepare the situation spiritually. Isn't that the result we want from the education we provide? It's our responsibility and duty as Catholic educators to give these children every opportunity to learn aspects of their faith to draw from in the many situations and challenges of life.

If you don't have holy water in your school, in all the classrooms, the lunchroom, the library, etc., get some! Teach about it, use it, and give them opportunities to use it.

Create a Mindset and Spirit of Service

It is very easy to become so focused on ourselves and what we are doing that we neglect developing a spirit of service and a recognition for the needs that exist beyond our boundaries. From a very young age, children should learn to give of themselves, to help others, to recognize when a need exists and do what they can to help fill that need. It starts as simple as helping mom or dad do a job or comforting or helping a younger sibling. By school age, children need to learn to look for needs that exist in the people around them—a task they could do for a teacher, a classmate who needs help or looks sad, a gesture to help keep their school clean and orderly, etc. Then it needs to extend into looking beyond their own borders. They need to know that there are those beyond their four walls that are hurting and need help. A very simple way to begin exposing them to meeting that need could be a monthly "service week." When I was the principal in an elementary Catholic school, we did just that. The last week of every month was "service week," and we partnered with a local charity to provide for their expressed needs in our community. Each day had a focus, and we would all participate in each day's theme.

For example, it was something like:

- Money Monday—Children brought money of any amount for the charity's needs.
- Tissue Tuesday—Children brought Kleenex, toilet paper, and paper towels for the charity.
- Wash-up Wednesday—Items for cleansing (shampoo, soap, etc.).
- Toothpaste Thursday—Toothpaste, toothbrushes, floss.
- Food Friday—Canned goods, boxed meals.

In December we really stepped it up and had "service week" every week leading up to Christmas. I sincerely believe it really helped us all keep our perspective more focused on others rather than solely on ourselves as so easily happens during the holidays.

The amount of money and needed items provided astounded the charity. We kept them stocked throughout the year! As children become older the service activities expand and change based on their abilities and interests. Once again, just seek God and creative ideas will flow!

Become a Community of Celebration

I close out this chapter with some thoughts regarding the climate of our Catholic schools. Having been in many, I would have to say that a true, consistent, celebratory atmosphere of our Catholic faith is difficult to find. So many Catholic schools just feel like every other school except that there are religious symbols on the walls and a few practices to exhibit its Catholic heritage. We have the greatest thing going! We have the privilege of educating young minds through the lens of our rich Catholic heritage. Let's celebrate that! Let's create a culture that is undeniably Catholic in every way. Let's resurrect beautiful traditions and fill our building with prayer, and we will see the power and presence of the Holy Spirit in ways we never could have imagined! Our culture is so hurried, so devoid of meaningful, rich celebrations. We must do something about it!

Throughout the calendar of the Church year we have so many opportunities to celebrate, reflect, and ponder. Our time belongs to God. To help us experience this more fully, the Catholic Church marks the passage of time with a cycle of seasons and feasts that invites us, year after year, to deepen our relationship with Jesus. We have saints to get to know and feast days to celebrate. We have Advent and Christmas, Lent, the Triduum, and Easter. We have Holy Days of Obligation and years of special focus designated by our pope. There are times to rejoice and times to repent. We have it all, but we fall so short of allowing this rhythm within the Church to touch our lives and help direct our paths.

In a book titled *Sacred Time and the Search for Meaning*, by Gary Eberle, the essence of our need for these sacred celebrations is eloquently stated.

> So the celebration of a ritual, which is another way of saying the experience of sacred time, is the celebration of all life, the quotidian ways we earn our daily bread and also all those other elements of existence that extend beyond the mere struggle to survive. In the end, entering the sacred time through prayer, meditation, ritual, or festival is a way of saying yes to all life. The well performed celebration leaves us saying, "Yes, life is worth living in spite of all the suffering connected with it." The affirmation of life is possible because in the ritual festive moment we touch an eternity that knows no privation. By exiting profane time and entering the liminal realm of sacred time, we shift our mental focus from the hurried

world of our everyday lives and enter another rhythm, larger than our individual lives or even our society.[7]

Don't we all desperately need that? Isn't it possible that our attention to the rhythm of the Church and the opportunities available to celebrate and reflect could produce in us a peace and clarity so lacking in our society? Isn't it worth a try? The opportunities are endless when it comes to introducing our children to this way of thinking. There are books available filled with ideas, but once you begin earnestly working towards creating a culture celebrating faith ideas will come randomly and naturally. Our schools are filled with talented, creative individuals whose talents would come alive in such a culture. Trust that!

Finally, if this all seems a little overwhelming and you are well into a school year or just feel like you can't possibly make all these adjustments, just choose one thing and begin to implement it regularly. Together as a community, do it prayerfully and faithfully. Once you feel that one thing is moving along well, add another thing. It's a process, and each one should be done intentionally and with excellence before adding something new. Our God is a God of excellence, and He will honor and bless our efforts. We will have time we didn't think we had, and room will become available within our schedules—kind of like the loaves and the fishes!

7. Eberle, *Sacred Time*.

Grace for You and Grace for Me

From Webster's *American Dictionary of the English Language,*
1828:

> **GRACE**, *noun* (Latin *gratia*, which is formed on the
> Celtic; Eng. agree, congruous, and ready. The primary
> sense of *gratus* is free, ready, quick, willing, prompt, from
> advancing.) Favor; good will; kindness; disposition to
> oblige another; as a grant made as an act of *grace*.[1]

Grace. As I reflect back on my years in education—public
education, Christian education, Catholic education—one thing I
have experienced as a real deficit in our school communities is
a lack of grace. Looking at the above definition we see the words
"free," "ready," "quick," "willing," "prompt," "favor," "good will,"
"kindness," "disposition to oblige another." I reflect on these words
with a sense of sadness at the opportunities missed within our
schools to teach the reception of grace from God and the exten-
sion of grace to one another.

All you have to do is look around you, in your workplace, in
your churches, in your neighborhoods, in shopping malls, grocery
stores, airports, even your own living rooms and within your own
immediate and extended families, and you can find evidence of
a lack of grace. We live in a time where the unending search for
self-satisfaction has taken ahold of our lives. As a society, we have
become obsessed with success—educational success, professional
success, athletic success, and the list goes on. As our lives become

1. Webster, *American Dictionary*, "Grace."

more empty spiritually, we strive to fill the emptiness with a desire for recognition, material goods, experiences, physical wellbeing, relationships, and this list goes on as well. It is a futile effort that ultimately leads to emptiness, despair, and at times destructive behaviors, because the cup is always only half-full. It always falls short when it is focused on the wrong things, the wrong ideals, the wrong approaches. These efforts, though good in appearance and satisfying for a time, fall short in our lives, because it all revolves around "me." We can't acquire grace, we can only first receive it as a gift from God, then extend it to those around us. It comes back to us as we share it. "Give and there will be gifts for you: a full measure pressed down, shaken together and overflowing will be poured into your lap; because the standard you use will be the standard used for you" (Luke 6:38, NJB).

This mentality goes totally against the way we generally function, which is "once my needs are met, I will have time for others." Really? Seeking to fulfill our own needs, our own success, our own happiness, only results in feeling like a bottomless pit. We may feel a sense of accomplishment or happiness at what we have acquired, but very soon it will all fade again into that sense that something is missing. That something missing is the grace of God realized in our own life, then given to those around us. First we must recognize that we are nothing without Christ, and that we deserve nothing. Once we come to terms with that we are ready to recognize God's grace and receive His grace freely. Then, with that in mind, we can now see that just as we are frail and in desperate need of God, so is everyone else. No longer are we better than anyone, we are on a level playing field, all sinners, all in need of God's grace, and all invited to receive it with one stipulation—that grace is only as powerful as our willingness to share it.

Think about your home, schools you have been a part of, your church, your extended family, etc. Think about times when strife has existed and be very honest about what you see. Isn't it there because somewhere along the line "we" was replaced with "me"? Since this is a book about education, take a moment and pause and reflect on your school community now or one you have been a part of in the past. Think about the challenges you have experienced or witnessed in regards to students, parents, colleagues, a pastor, a school board, a secretary, or other school employees. How many conversations have you overheard about challenging students, difficult parents, a stubborn principal or pastor, an insensitive school board? How many of those conversations have you not only heard, but how many have you openly participated in? What happens in the privacy of your teacher's lounge? What happens when the principal changes something and some of the staff don't like it? What things get talked about in hallways and behind closed doors in classrooms when someone wants to share their displeasure? How many parents linger in parking lots discussing their dislike of a certain teacher, principal, or policy? I think we could all agree that we have both witnessed and at times probably have participated in these situations. It really doesn't take much thought to recognize how desperately we need the transforming grace of God in our communities—the grace we receive from Him and the grace we must then extend out.

Receiving that grace takes us back to where we started in this book. It takes us back to the decision to seek that personal relationship with Christ, giving Him everything and asking Him to take control. Once we do that it is without question that He has extended His grace to us. Once we have humbled ourselves in that regard, we in essence have said yes to receiving that grace. So once we have it, what is the next step? Well, the next step is realizing that though we didn't deserve it, it was given, and though those around us may not deserve grace from us, it still must be given. That's how it works in God's economy. He gives it as a gift and intends for it to transform us so that it can be extended and transform others and draw others to Him.

Now what would happen if we all tried to the best of our ability to do that? What would happen if we took this very seriously and tried very hard to begin implementing a spirit of grace in our relationships and our situations at school? Would our lunch conversations change, would parking lot conversations change, would our descriptions of our administrators and coworkers change?

If not—then we have missed the point! We live in a very critical and "me-centered" culture. Believing the best of others is not the norm. Our media surrounds us with stories of criticism and anger, our politicians attack one another viciously, our government lacks civility and cooperation, our churches have elements we distrust, etc. It's no wonder it is so ingrained in us and colors so many aspects of our personal and professional lives. That's why the Church has to lead in this. We can look to the Saints, to popes throughout history, and other outstanding leaders within the Church as prime examples of those who desire to exhibit and live a spirit of grace and mercy for us to emulate. As well, our Catholic schools should be a beacon of light in this regard.

As Catholic educators it is our duty to create and preserve an atmosphere of faith and learning that exhibits the love of God and His grace for everyone. We are only fooling ourselves if we think that the children in our care don't pick up on our dislike or disapproval of someone or something in our community. Just as children in a home know when mom and dad are in unity or not, so do they sense unity or a lack of it in school. Perhaps in a public school it is not as noticeable, but it is not the mission of a public school to train a child in principles of faith; it is OUR mission, and one that should be at the top of our list.

So, how do we begin to take back lost ground in this area? Ideally, it should begin at the top, with the pastor, if it is a parish-sponsored school. In choosing or mentoring a principal or other administrators within the school, the pastor should take the lead. He should be aware of the personality of his leaders and charge them with the importance of setting the example in this area for the school. If the pastor is uninvolved or does not take this lead, is everyone off the hook? Clearly the answer is no! Then I would say to the principal and other leadership in the school, "Even without the leadership or involvement of the pastor, you must lead." Developing a spirit of grace isn't dependent on who around us or in charge of us is doing it first. It really doesn't matter. What matters is that those recognizing that it is missing be the ones to step out and begin making it happen. It is better if it starts at the top, but it is not required.

Principals and administrators—this should be a top priority for you! Over and above every bit of planning should be an evaluation of the level of grace present in your community. It should be reflected in your hiring, in your mentoring, in your planning, and in your review of programs and people. It should be so important to you that you are willing to make changes in plans, programs, and people to make it a priority. And to be very honest, if as a principal or administrator you do not see the relevance and connection, then perhaps you need to reevaluate your role in that school community. It is not fair for those in the community to suffer a lack of spiritual direction because of your unwillingness to change, submit, or be a channel of that grace. Maybe your educational gifts could be better utilized in a public or charter school setting. As a Catholic school leader you have the responsibility to be the very best CATHOLIC spiritual leader you can be. If, for whatever reason, you can't do that, maybe it's best you move on and leave the door open for someone who can and wants to. I'm sorry if that seems harsh, but it's the truth. You don't have to be perfect, just humble and willing to change and grow. If not, be honest about it—there's too much at stake.

Faculty and staff—this should be a top priority for you!

And what if you don't have a pastor or administrator making this a priority? Does it change your responsibility? Of course not. You can have a huge impact as a staff and can literally change the course of the environment of your school if together, even without leadership from the top, you work to create a grace-filled, loving community. I might really be dating myself, but do you remember the old Disney movie *Pollyanna*? One girl transformed a community through the little things she did to bring joy and a new perspective to those around her. Don't ever underestimate the power of the Holy Spirit working through willing, faithful individuals.

Parents—this should be a top priority for you! In this category, however, I take a slightly different approach. Though I firmly believe parents have a responsibility to uphold and maintain principles of faith in the schools of their children, and though I think parents can greatly damage a school atmosphere with negativity and critical attitudes, first and foremost I believe parents have a responsibility to choose the very best spiritual and educational atmosphere for their children. A child spends seven-plus hours a day in a school setting and as primary educators of their children parents hold the ultimate responsibility of choosing very carefully who oversees those seven-plus hours a day. If a good academic education is all you are worried about, yes, Catholic schools are really good at providing strong academics. But if you sincerely value and care about the things I have been sharing and you don't see it clearly apparent in a particular Catholic school that you are considering, I would suggest you look elsewhere, and if you are already in a school and it is clear that an authentic spirit of faith and grace is not a priority, then again I would suggest you look elsewhere. There is only so much influence you can have in an environment where you are not present throughout the day. You get one chance at this task of educating your children and preparing them for life spiritually and academically. Don't waste this time because it's convenient, your friends go there, etc. This is the most important responsibility of your life. Hold those you are enlisting to assist you accountable, and if they won't respond—move on!

But . . . if you have found such a place, then you have the equal responsibility of being a positive support and extender of grace. Your involvement and support is necessary and crucial. Don't drop your children off each day and forget to pray for, assist, and encourage these men and women who are helping to raise your children. They are not your employees, they are your partners. And I will say, as I stated to teachers, if you are not necessarily looking for a strong element of faith, then perhaps you would fit better at a public or charter school. Lukewarm parents can negatively affect a school culture. Many times, I have heard parents say, "My focus is their academics—the faith aspect is not all that important to me." How sad to be more concerned for the development of their minds and forgo the development of their hearts and spirits. I understand the concern for the temporal, but how much more concerned should they be for the eternal destination of their children?

Authority—Who Needs It?

Who needs authority? WE DO!
  Who says? GOD!

> Everyone is to obey governing authorities, because there is no authority except from God and so whatever authorities exist have been appointed by God. So anyone who disobeys an authority is rebelling against God's ordinance; and rebels must expect to receive the condemnation they deserve.

> —Romans 13:7 (NJB)

> I urge, then, first of all that petitions, prayers, intercessions, and thanksgiving should be offered for everyone, for kings and others in authority, so that we may be able to live peaceful and quiet lives with all devotion and propriety. To do this is right, and acceptable to God our Savior: He wants everyone to be saved and reach full knowledge of the truth.

> —1 Timothy 2:1–3 (NJB)

> Remind them to be obedient to the officials in authority; to be ready to do good at every opportunity; not to go slandering other people but to be peaceable and gentle, and always polite to people of all kinds.

> —Titus 3:1 (NJB)

> For the sake of the Lord, accept the authority of every human institution: the emperor, as the supreme authority, and the governors as commissioned by him to punish criminals and praise those who do good. It is God's will that by your good deeds you should silence the ignorant talk of fools. You are slaves of no one except God, so behave like free people, and never use your freedom as a cover for wickedness. Have respect for everyone and love for your fellow believers; fear God and honor the emperor.

—1 Peter 2:13–17 (NJB)

There is probably no need to add another Scripture, but I add this final one—a favorite of mine.

> Obey your leaders and give way to them; they watch over your souls because they must give an account of them; make this a joy for them to do, and not a grief—you yourselves would be the losers.

—Hebrews 13:17 (NJB)

It is so clear that God values obedience. Scripture states, "Has the Lord as great delight in burnt offerings and sacrifices, as in obedience to the voice of the Lord? Surely, to obey is better than sacrifice, and to heed than the fat of rams" (1 Sam 15:22, NRSV).

First the requirement is obedience to God and His word, then obedience to those placed in authority, as is so evident in the Scriptures above. I love how the passage in 1 Peter states how not heeding this directive from God would cause us to "be the losers." And isn't that the truth! Who wins when there is disunity, discord, rebellion against authority? No one wins! The leader is miserable, those he/she leads are unsettled, and in the case of a school community—everyone knows and feels what's going on. People want to be a part of a winning team, and a winning team is an orderly, positive, grace-filled team. A winning team is one where ignorant, destructive conversation and attitudes are silenced. A winning team is one that does not allow the attempts of the evil one to infiltrate and take residence in a community of faith. Will the leader always be right? Of course not. But those under that leader will always be right if they give that leader the benefit of the doubt, and ultimately get in step with the directives of that leader. I firmly believe that when a leader is off-target on something, he/she will realize it much more quickly if a supportive staff, after sharing sincere concerns, vows to trust and uphold that leader's decision. Of course, here we are NOT talking about something that goes against the spiritual mission of the school or would be dangerous, harmful, or negligent to the community. We are talking about the many decisions that people bicker over or refuse to follow just because they think their idea is better. As someone who has been on both sides, as a teacher and as an administrator, I have witnessed and participated in the perspective of both. And I will say that I understood much better how important the principles of the above Scriptures were once I was in administration. When you are carrying the weight and burden of leadership for a community and you are sincerely trying to follow God and be faithful to His will for that community, dealing with stubborn, opinionated staff or parents can come close to crippling your ability to lead. Leadership is a lonely spot: there are so many reasons for people to question you, disagree with you, and challenge you, and usually it is because what you are recommending is challenging to them or may shake up their "it's always been done this way" mentality.

God is dynamic and wants His people to be dynamic as well, but being dynamic is not comfortable or easy. Being dynamic requires that we have a prayerful spirit, an open heart, and an open mind so we can access God's perspective. It usually requires that we sacrifice a little more, that we work a little harder, learn a little more, compromise more, and set aside our preconceived notions about things. It requires more prayer, more patience, more resilience and perseverance and our selfish nature doesn't want to do those things. So . . . we cling to what we have known, what is comfortable and requires the least of us. Quite a prescription for mediocrity, wouldn't you say?

So try it!

Principals, honor your leadership—your pastor, your superintendent, and anyone else who is in a leadership position over you.

Be trustworthy, positive, and hopeful. Pray for your leadership and develop a healthy, respectful relationship with those people. Let them know where you may disagree with them, but assure them that you desire to honor God's mandate regarding leadership and that you can be trusted to obey.

Teachers, honor your principal. Get in line and let him or her know you are there to honor God's directive regarding his/her leadership.

Do not allow a negative word to proceed from your mouth regarding your principal/administrator. Any issues you may have, take to prayer and seal your lips from speaking discord. This means avoiding those hallway or private classroom chats with other staff, guarding your words in the teacher's lounge, protecting your leader's reputation with parents and others in the school community. It means praying for your leader and taking any concerns or questions directly to that person, trusting that God will touch his/her heart and guide them in responding to those concerns appropriately. And if you don't get the result you had hoped for, practice the virtues of patience and trust. Continue to support and build that relationship and avenues of dialogue, and watch God move.

Parents, again—choose your school carefully and vow to pray for, support, and encourage the leadership and staff within the school. Guard yourselves in those tempting situations, such as the parking lot, the internet, and social gatherings. Avoid running to the pastor or the board with complaints and disagreements, and instead go directly to the person you have a concern with. Talk openly and charitably, but keep an open mind to the fact that what you see or perceive is usually a very small aspect of a very big picture. Give those in leadership in your school (including teachers) the benefit of the doubt and the gift of mercy and grace, and teach your children to do the same. School communities are made up of many different personalities and life stories. There are pains and difficulties we don't know about. When we look at things only from our perspective we miss huge opportunities to extend grace and compassion, and instead we inflict more pain and judgment, and we build walls rather than bridges.

No one wins when everyone is looking out for themselves and their interests, but everyone ultimately wins when a community tries hard (though imperfectly at times) to honor God's desire for unity, respect, and obedience. It is in the difficulties and sometimes lengthy processes involved in working through our differences that the Holy Spirit can work most powerfully. Sometimes resolutions to issues take MUCH longer because of our stubbornness and unwillingness to trust, support, and uphold the authority in our lives. God never gets it wrong! If we do it His way, He will, in His time, allow us to benefit from the fruits of that obedience. And I say all this without having mentioned the great gift such a mindset will have on our children. They will learn to conduct themselves in this manner if we model it, teach it, and hold fast to it. Imagine the life lessons for a child who in the midst of a struggle with an adult or another child at a school is taught to pray for that person, to recognize the good in them, to do good for them, and to trust that God will "work all things together for good." Imagine the power of them seeing how their faithfulness to God's principles bears fruit in their lives and in the lives of others! What a priceless gift, to encourage a healthy sense of self-esteem in a child. When we teach them to be "other-centered" we teach them to not take the little discouragements or disappointments of life so seriously and so personally. We teach them to stay above the gutter, to trust in God for their self-worth instead of the constantly changing opinions of others. We give them a strength of character and resolve that will keep them sturdy and resilient.

As I write this it strikes me what a sharp contrast this is to what we currently see in the youth of today, who lack that understanding and faith in God's ways that we have been talking about. I am writing this chapter a week after the presidential election of 2016. This was an election that has had me glued to the TV. There has never been an election that has brought me more anxiety or has created more of an urgency to prayer. From my perspective so much was at stake—the abortion issue, the Supreme Court, and the overall direction of our nation. I watched every speech, read every article I came across, and researched all that I could so that I could be informed. My husband and I prayed a rosary a night for this election for several months before November 8 and we were comforted hearing about prayer being front and center in so many areas of our country. I will admit that as the votes were starting to come in and states were being called I felt a sense of heaviness and concern that maybe the media was right and maybe the outcome was inevitable, but at least I knew I had done all I could. I knew we took this very seriously and that we prayed diligently and I had high hopes that many others did as well. I will also admit (probably to some people's irritation) that as I sat up until three in the morning to hear who had been elected that I began to thank God for having heard those prayers. I don't know in the end how it will all turn out with this new administration, but I will continue to pray and remain hopeful that some of the most important issues, beginning with life, that maybe we have been given a chance to get this right.

So as I got up the next morning, more hopeful than I had been since the start of the election cycle, I soon watched on TV how out-of-control those who had not gotten the result they wanted had become. Even my daughter, who teaches in a Catholic school, was surrounded by people devastated at the election results. She was afraid to say who she had voted for. How could that be, in a Catholic school where the protection of life should be a top priority? I listened with dismay at the reports of college exams and classes being cancelled, rooms being set up with therapy dogs, Play-Doh, and crayons to help young people cope. I watched with great sadness at cities being damaged by protesters while signs were displayed stating "Not My President." This display and response of people and youth who had not gotten their way, to me, exhibited clearly the result of a "me-centered" culture rebellious towards authority. It showed me how desperately needed are Catholic schools dedicated to displaying, encouraging, and living the principles of faith we have been talking about. We have to reclaim a sense of respect and obedience for authority. We need to teach, model, and practice these virtues and principles daily and with serious determination. Our communities need to be a light and a guide for our youth. What will be the result if we don't heed this warning and mandate? I think we all know.

So as you ponder the climate and atmosphere of your school community, be honest and begin a discussion. Be transparent about the areas that need work, be determined to change directions, and pray diligently for the grace and power of the Holy Spirit in your endeavor. We are fighting against a very strong, established tide of individualism and rebellion. It is going to require a boldness and courage that only God can provide to stand in the face of the fight. It will take some time, but will be well worth the fight. Not only will you be aiding the transformation of your community as you place serious emphasis on what matters most to God, but you also will be raising up a generation of children better equipped to stand in the face of the efforts of evil in our world.

A dear friend who also happens to be in religious life shared with me recently something her brother said to her after twenty-five years of being estranged from her and her sister. As this friend prayed fervently for her brother all those years, she trusted that God would answer those prayers somehow, and came to accept that it could be that she would never see him again in this life. But out of the blue one day he called and asked her to forgive him for all the time that had passed. She asked him what changed his mind and he said that he heard someone say one day, "Do you want to be happy or be right?" He decided to stop being so stubborn and self-righteous and chose instead to be happy and be reunited with his sisters! How profound!

In your life and in your school—where are you fighting to be right? Choose instead to be happy! The world needs more happiness—let it start with you!

Speak Life

I NAMED THIS CHAPTER "Speak Life," inspired by the words of a song entitled "Speak Life," by Toby Mac. I encourage you to look up the lyrics and read them—pull up the song and listen to them again being sung. Consider carefully their meaning and the promise of hope that accompanies carefully chosen speech. How true these verses are in regard to our personal lives and within our schools!

Life will always be a mix of it all—the good, the bad, the right, the wrong, and everything in between, but Christ made it very clear that our words and our perspective make all the difference as we respond to our ever-changing, sometimes very difficult circumstances.

As educators the following verse speaks very directly to our hearts:

> Not many of you should become teachers, my brothers and sisters, for you know that we who teach will be judged with greater strictness. For all of us make many mistakes. Anyone who makes no mistakes in speaking is perfect, able to keep the whole body in check with a bridle. If we put bits into the mouths of horses to make them obey us, we guide their whole bodies. Or look at ships: though they are so large that it takes strong winds to drive them, yet they are guided by a very small rudder wherever the will of the pilot directs. So also the tongue is a small member, yet it boasts of great exploits.
>
> How great a forest is set ablaze by a small fire! And the tongue is a fire. The tongue is placed among our

members as a world of iniquity; it stains the whole body, sets on fire the cycle of nature, and is itself set on fire by hell. For every species of beast and bird, of reptile and sea creature, can be tamed and has been tamed by the human species, but no one can tame the tongue—a restless evil, full of deadly poison. With it we bless the Lord and Father, and with it we curse those who are made in the likeness of God. From the same mouth come blessing and cursing. My brothers and sisters, this ought not to be so. Does a spring pour forth from the same opening both fresh and brackish water? Can a fig tree, my brothers and sisters, yield olives, or a grapevine figs? No more can salt water yield fresh.

—James 3:1–12 (NRSV)

How interesting that God addresses teachers in this long discourse on the tongue and the damage that it can do. Clearly He considers the teacher's role as critical in passing along and modeling truth or passing along and modeling evil. Our words make a difference! They set the tone and direct the spirit of the community. They are heard, overheard, and repeated. Once spoken, the effect of our words cannot be reversed—not even with an apology. If they were unkind, judgmental, or evil, the effects can remain even if we try to reverse them. Harsh, critical words hurt, they damage, they destroy confidence, they kill hope, and they start a flame that can get out of control.

How often in a school community do you hear or overhear comments about children, comments about parents, the principal, another teacher, the pastor, the superintendent, the bishop, the pope, etc.? Everyone likes to think they are right, everyone likes to feel they are in the know, that they have a better idea or see a situation clearly. And maybe sometimes they do—but if these things are spoken with the wrong motive, with pride, resentment, or anger, they begin a course of destruction and evil.

What if a common goal in a school community was to "speak life"? What if, in the midst of disagreement, a comment was kept back, rather than pushed forward? What if a staff and faculty trained itself to refrain from negative comments about any students, parents, or others within the community? What if staff and faculty were willing to hold each other accountable to speaking only life? What if students in a classroom frequently heard words of life spoken over themselves and their fellow students? What if they were taught daily to look for the good in others and were given opportunities to speak those things out openly and in the hearing of others? What if parents were received with grace in the midst of conflict and were always greeted with words of life before an issue or disagreement was addressed? What if we were busy using words of life to spark fires of grace, forgiveness, humility, and patience? Would your school be a different place? Wouldn't you be providing a life skill for your students that would guide them their entire life? Imagine the impact—an impact that could go on for generations!

There is nothing in our way to stop us but ourselves. What if you are in a pretty negative environment? Well, I would say that truth only needs a spark to set the fire ablaze. Can you be that spark, can you be the one who sets the example and refuses to engage, one who gently encourages your students and others to do the same? It has to begin somewhere and with someone. Preferably, it would be best to have it start from the top down, but if it doesn't, there is nothing holding you back. Do what's right and trust the results to the Holy Spirit. He won't let you down! This is where your personal prayer life and patience is essential. Take your frustrations to the Lord and ask for the strength to be that light in the midst of darkness. Your light may be the exact reason God has you placed where you are! Don't fall prey to going through the motions and just doing a job—make where you are planted a mission field and set those around you ablaze!

This is clearly a topic that should be a focus of the professional prayer life of the community. We are all subject to fatigue, frustration, and discouragement. We have to call these things by name and together pray through them, then turn to Scripture and practice responding to situations scripturally instead of being led by our emotions. God will be faithful!

In a time when so many of our Catholic schools struggle to stay afloat this principle is more important than ever, because the enemy is alive and well, looking for any open door to bring destruction to our communities of faith. Let me share a very brief story as an example. Recently I visited a friend who is a principal and had just moved to another state to become principal of a "highly regarded" Catholic school. He arrived full of hope and anticipation of a great community only to be met with a disgruntled influential parent. The parent apparently had an issue with someone in leadership slightly connected with the school community. This person the parent was frustrated with had no direct influence over anything that occurred in the school, but the parent couldn't let it go and began to spread this frustration and build a case. Before you knew it many families were involved, and you can only imagine how details and descriptions changed as it was passed from one person to another. By the time it was all said and done forty families were disgruntled and made a choice to leave the school! Imagine the impact on the children, on the community, on the faculty, the staff, and the administration. Imagine the inaccurate perspective that leaked out into the public. These types of things should not be happening in our schools. We have been charged with the responsibility to train up this next generation. What did that accomplish, except to damage a school and set an example that if you don't like something you just leave and get as many on your side as possible? Imagine the implications of that example in the lives of the children who witnessed it. What do they have to refer to when they are in a situation they don't agree with, in a marriage that is not going so well, in a family struggle, etc.? We MUST consider the implications of our example, our responses, and our decisions in dealing with conflict. If we approach it from God's perspective in Scripture, we have hope for a good outcome. If we resort to our emotions, our rights, our perspective, we can be assured that we are entering dangerous territory.

What will we choose as educators, even if we feel like the minority?

I will close with a list of Scriptures referencing the importance of our words. Take some time and go through them by yourself, as a staff, and with your students. Ponder them, discuss them, and begin working to put these principles in action in your life and in your school.

Proverbs 11:9
Proverbs 11:12
Proverbs 11:17
Proverbs 12:18
Proverbs 13:3
Proverbs 15:1
Proverbs 15:4
Proverbs 16:24
Proverbs 18:4
Proverbs 18:21
Proverbs 20:15
Proverbs 25:18
Matthew 12:33–37
Ephesians 4:29
James 3:5–8
SPEAK LIFE!

Pursue Excellence!

Whatever your work is, put your heart into it as done for the Lord and not for human beings, knowing that the Lord will repay you by making you His heirs. It is Christ the Lord you are serving.

—COLOSSIANS 3:23–24 (NJB)

IMAGINE IF YOU COULD physically see Jesus Christ present in your school each day—imagine that any moment He could walk into any classroom, any meeting, any planning sessions—that He could overhear any conversation, would know how well prepared you are for the children you serve, etc. What would you change—what would be different?

I think without a doubt we all would do some things differently if we could see Jesus present in our schools each day. And the truth is—He is there each and every day! We don't physically see Him, but we know He is present. What if we took that truth and applied it as a measuring stick for all that we do?

How would that affect you as an employee? Would you hit the snooze button several times in the morning and risk arriving late to school? Would you begin a day of instruction or administrative oversight less than fully prepared? Would you gossip? Would you snap at a student? Would you criticize a parent or discuss the shortcomings of a student with others? Of course, we are all frail human beings prone to making mistakes, but are there some things we can do in a practical sense to help us stay on course or get back on course quickly if we fall off?

Be disciplined in your life.

First—take care of yourself. Make sure you have time set aside each day to pray before you leave the house. Perhaps make listening to Christian music on your ride into work a priority to set the stage for your perspective for the day. Eat well, get exercise and fresh air. Get a good night's sleep, and organize your time in a way that leaves you some breathing room for getting ready in the morning. Try to always make arriving to work a little earlier than required a goal. Set technology limits for yourself and hold to them.

Second—be prepared! When you make it a priority to be prepared for your days, things naturally go more smoothly. Being unprepared leaves an open door for the evil one to pounce at the first opportunity he sees to unravel you. What does it feel like when you arrive to school unprepared, trusting that copies can be made when you get there, that demonstrations can get set up during a special class, etc., and then the copier is down, or the specials teacher doesn't come in, and you now are without that time to do last-minute preparations? Not only do we become unsettled but so do our students. It's not that difficult of a problem to solve; it just takes determination and commitment. In the first school where I was principal we had a policy that we faithfully followed. Since I taught classes as well as served as principal it applied to me as well. It was required that every teacher was thoroughly planned for the following week before they left school on Friday for the weekend. Some teachers chose to stay after school on Friday to finish up plans for the next week and some did a little bit each day leading up to Friday, but regardless of how they accomplished this requirement each and every one of us left for the weekend knowing that all plans for the next week were complete and turned into the office, materials were prepared, and necessary copies were made. What this did was put us all in a mindset to prepare in advance, and it also gave us breathing room for the weekend. Instead of going home having the planning for the following week hanging over our heads and sometimes not getting completed until Sunday, we all left knowing we were ready and free to do what we should do on weekends—enjoy some rest, some fun with loved ones, and free to truly honor the Sabbath! We avoided the pitfall of an unexpected event during the weekend keeping us from planning and going into the next week scrambling. Being unprepared sets you up for stress and less-than-excellence in what you do. In addition, it left us as a school prepared in the event a teacher became ill or unable to come in for some reason. We had plans in place at least for the following week.

Please allow me to divert back to something I shared in the previous paragraph regarding honoring the Sabbath. Without spending too much time on this topic I would like to mention just a few things that will clearly date me but I sincerely feel are significant. As a young girl growing up in the 1960s Sundays always stood out in our home and community. There were natural guidelines in place that encouraged people—actually forced them in some cases—to slow down and unwind. For example, when I was young Saturday was our shopping day—meat market, grocery store, etc., because when Sunday came just about everything was closed. There were no malls, grocery stores, or gas stations open. Almost everything else that involved retail of any kind was closed. My mother hung laundry outside to dry in nice weather, and every Saturday my dad took down the clothes line so it wasn't up on Sunday, and then he put it back up on Monday. As silly and unnecessary this may sound it left such an image in my mind of the sacredness of the Lord's Day. This pause in the week caused you to plan for your needs to be taken care of on Saturday or before, and when Sunday came many people were seen leaving their homes to go to church. Attending church was a focus for many families! Can we say that today? Is church the main event or one of many events for the day? Are we able, in this overstimulated culture, to slow down enough to take in the beauty of this time—this Sabbath—as a day of spiritual refreshment, rest, and relaxation? If not, I believe we are truly missing something essential for our lives. This mindset of Sabbath produced other important things in our lives.

Sunday family dinners were more frequent. Neighbors were often outside; they visited and sometimes shared meals or just casual conversation on a porch or in a backyard. There was time to read, to cook, to ride bikes, play ball, or just do nothing. I believe with all my heart that it was healthy for us all.

In a favorite article I read several years back written by a Jewish woman, Allegra Goodman, "And on the Seventh Day, She Rests: Hardworking Modern Woman Celebrates the Restorative Power of the Sabbath," the author states,

> We all tell ourselves the benefits of rest. Without enough rest, body and mind malfunction. Without enough sleep, personalities fray. Free time and relaxation are all necessary for productivity. But Shabbat is not a utilitarian ritual. It is not a stratagem for getting more done, but an end in itself. In the Jewish tradition, after God created the world, He rested on the seventh day. Therefore, when we observe the Sabbath, we imitate God. We were made in His image, and now we stretch to imitate His act. This spiritual stretching is the sweetest part of Shabbat. On this day, a mother can liberate herself from time, and like a kid forgo wearing a watch. Parents and children can enjoy one another free from the burdens of the school and social calendar. Above all, a working grown-up can celebrate the freedom to sit back and just be.[1]

As Catholics if we were to cherish the Sabbath as a day for both spiritual and personal refreshment, how would our lives be enhanced? Could you benefit from paying closer attention to how you can create and honor the Sabbath in your life and the life of your family? Would you come to work on Monday more fulfilled, more ready to reach out to those you serve, and more in touch with what Christ is doing in your life? Doesn't it make you wonder? Unfortunately, the natural barriers in our society of things being shut down on Sundays no longer exists, but we can create our own barriers and hold to them.

---

1. Goodman, "And on the Seventh Day," 24.

Third—remain humble. By this I mean be very cautious about falling into the trap that you are in any way better than anyone else. This can creep up in unexpected ways, especially if we are trying to pursue excellence, be better prepared, take better care of ourselves. It can become very easy to look around you and notice that others are not putting in all the effort that you are and before you know it you begin to judge, criticize, and make comparisons. The call to pursue excellence is an individual one between us and God. It is to our advantage and everyone else's if we stay focused on ourselves, gently encourage others when a door is open, but guarding carefully the temptation to judge. What an amazing transformation could occur in a school if everyone attempted to make some of these adjustments, and that should be our goal, but the truth is that probably not everyone will. Just try to remain humble and stay focused so that God can use your example as a light instead of a measuring stick.

Fourth—pursue excellence in the relationships around you. Always remember that everyone has a story. A perceived cold shoulder from someone doesn't always mean rudeness, but could rather be the result of something painful going on in their life. Falling short in an area doesn't always mean an unwillingness to do things a certain way but could mean an insecurity or a fear of failure. This holds true with colleagues, students, parents, and those in leadership. We are all on a journey and we all need support. Be that support. Do your best to keep your spirit and heart open to what the Holy Spirit may be trying to show you in your surroundings. Choose grace as your first response. God will always make trouble or concerns evident at which point someone will need to address it.

Fifth—be a loyal and trustworthy employee. Strive to be an employee that leadership always knows they can trust. Display your loyalty and trustworthiness as you support those in authority. Display it in avoiding getting involved in gossip or criticism. Be the employee that as a first course of action always goes directly to the source of any conflict or disagreement and avoids at all costs sharing those conflicts or disagreements with others. Be someone that can be counted on, approached, and trusted to always be looking out for the best interests of others.

So to close this chapter, remember that the pursuit of excellence is within your reach, but some things have to be in place for it to flow naturally from you.

Take care of yourself spiritually.

Take care of yourself physically.

Discipline yourself to be prepared for your responsibilities.

Carve a Sabbath mindset in your week.

Remain humble of heart.

Pursue excellence in your relationships.

Be a loyal and trustworthy person and employee.

These are all choices within your reach—reach high!

A Few More Things

Memorization—A Practice That for a Long Time Was Standard Practice in Schools

MANY OF YOU READING this book grew up memorizing things—nursery rhymes, songs, math, history facts, etc. But the truth is, this practice of memorization has become almost nonexistent in our lives and in our schools. The thinking is: who needs to memorize anything when so much information is available at your fingertips, why memorize math facts when calculators can do the work for you, why memorize historical facts and information—isn't all that useless and unimportant?

In an article I recently read on the site *TutorHunt* titled "In Praise of Memorization," some very practical information is shared regarding this fading practice. I've abbreviated the points from the article, but the basic premise of each makes sense and is worth serious consideration.[1]

1. Memorization trains your brain to remember—it's an exercise that gives your brain strength to retain information.

2. Memorization challenges your brain, just like a workout at the gym challenges your body.

3. Rote learning improves neural plasticity—something needed all through our lives.

1. TutorHunt, "In Praise of Memorization."

4. Memorization offers a mental gymnastics exercise, making your brain more quick and agile.

5. Memorization frees up brain power—when you already have information memorized (equations, definitions, etc.) you save brain power that can be used for other things.

6. Memorization helps students practice focus. When you think about it, where else are students required to practice focus? Everything is quick to access for them now.

7. Memorization is essential to learning new concepts—without a strong working memory comprehension is more difficult.

8. In small children memorization of nursery rhymes teaches rhythmic patterns, balance, and symmetry.

9. Memorization is important for creativity—the ability to focus and develop working memory can free a student's mind to be more creative.

10. Memorization can stave off cognitive decline. As the article relates: "Researchers from the National Institute on Health and Aging have found that adults who went through short bursts of memory training were better able to maintain higher cognitive functioning and everyday skills, even five years after going through the training. Practicing memorization allowed the elderly adults to delay typical cognitive decline by seven to fourteen years. Students who start practicing memory training now can stay sharp in years to come."

So in light of this consideration of the benefits of memory work, what can our schools do to bring back this skill? Well, at a very basic level we can again institute the practice of learning by memory things like math facts, spelling words, definitions, geography and history facts, as well as many other things. This can be done easily by building into the school day time to recite and repeat facts—it doesn't have to take a lot of extra time. It can be done for a couple minutes before a lesson begins, standing in line waiting to be dismissed, just about any time there are a free few minutes. This daily repetition of facts being learned is not just a benefit for ordinary students, but can be such an aid to struggling students as they hear over and over basic facts needing to be mastered.

As Catholic schools, I believe we have the opportunity and the responsibility to take this a step further. I know I already mentioned the importance of making sure Scripture is visible and taught in our Catholic schools, but I wanted to add another dimension to that topic.

"Do not be conformed to this world, but be transformed by the renewal of your mind so that you may discern what is the will of God—what is good and acceptable and perfect" (Rom 12:2, NRSV).

We are all surrounded by things attempting to conform us to this world—songs that are catchy with lyrics that are sketchy, video games, TV shows and lines in movies, stories, and books with messages that cause moral struggle in our hearts—numbing us to this culture. How do we confront this, how do we help our young people combat the barrage of messages that weaken a desire for holiness? I think memorization can play a big part! At a basic level, as teachers recognize the ease with which children learn lyrics to songs, an attempt could be made to make sure our schools are filled with beautiful, strong messages in music. There are so many options in Catholic and Christian music to expose to our children. They are naturally drawn to music—how profoundly could their hearts be touched by lyrics encouraging a love of God and a life of faith. What about poetry that gets tucked into their memory, able to be drawn out in the midst of struggle, confusion, or sorrow? Consider this first stanza from a five-stanza poem filled with encouragement to stay the course in tough times from Edgar A. Guest titled "Don't Quit":

> When Things go wrong, as they sometimes will,
> When the road you're trudging seems all uphill,
> When the funds are low and debts are high,
> And you want to Smile but have to sigh.
> When care is pressing you down a bit,
> Rest, if you must, but don't you quit.[2]

2. Guest, "Don't Quit," lines 1–6.

This is but a small example of the many, many poems accessible to us as parents and educators. We used many of Guest's poems in the Christian school my children attended. To this day, in their late twenties and early thirties, they can still recite stanzas from these poems, drawing a reminder to reach for higher things, loftier goals, and persevering through the challenges of life. What a gift to provide your students!

Most important is the practice of memorizing truth from God's Holy Word! God has given us the template for life in His word. We read it far too little, we know it far too little. We must bring it to life for ourselves and our students! It is our roadmap, our guide, our source of strength, hope, and encouragement. If we really understood that, it would never get dusty sitting on the shelves of our homes and classrooms. I recently heard a Christian leader say something to this effect: "Everyone wants a fresh word from God for their life, their situation, their challenges, their future. To that I respond—God gave us seventy-three books in His word! Read them, memorize them, and you will find your word!" There are so many things going on in our homes and classrooms that could be put aside to make room for more time spent in Scripture. But why memorize it? Well, consider these points regarding committing Scripture to memory.

- Jesus knew the word by heart and quoted it all the time. He is our model of the life-transforming power of using God's words instead of your own.

  Let the word of Christ dwell in you richly; teach and admonish one another in all wisdom; and with gratitude in your hearts sing psalms, hymns, and spiritual songs to God.

  —Colossians 3:16 (NRSV)

- It needs to live in us, fill us, be there at our disposal. Memorizing Scripture is not burdensome—it helps it dwell within us.

- Memorizing Scripture "renews our mind" and refreshes it from all the garbage thrown at us daily.

- It helps us in the midst of temptation. In Ephesians 6:10–20 we are given the weapons of our warfare against the enemy. Only one weapon is offensive—the sword of the Spirit—which is the Word of God. When temptation hits we don't always have the desire to or the luxury of sitting down and sifting through Scripture. We need it in our hearts, accessible through our memory, and ready as a sword against the temptations that come our way. What did Jesus use to fight temptation in the desert? Scripture!

- Helps us with obedience—"How can a young man keep his way pure? By guarding it according to your word" (Ps 119:9, NRSV).

- Keeps us open to blessing—"Blessed is the man who walks not in the counsel of the wicked, nor stands in the way of sinners, nor sits in the seat of scoffers; but his delight is in the law of the Lord, and on His law He meditates day and night" (Ps 1:1, NRSV).

- Memorizing Scripture gives us tools to more readily encourage others. Just like we don't always have the luxury of accessing Scripture in the midst of temptation, the same is true when we are faced with someone in need of encouragement or hope. If God's word is tucked away in our memory, the Holy Spirit can readily bring it to the forefront of our mind to share with someone at just the right time. But if it's not in there, we are left to our own words, which might be good, but will never compare with the power of God's words.

An old favorite Christian speaker and author from my days in the nondenominational world of faith, Chuck Swindoll, has written,

> I know of no other single practice in the Christian life more rewarding, practically speaking, then memorizing Scripture . . . No other single exercise pays greater spiritual dividends! Your prayer life will be strengthened.

> Your witnessing will be sharper and much more effective. Your attitudes and outlook will begin to change. Your mind will become alert and observant. Your confidence and assurance will be enhanced. Your faith will be solidified.[3]

As a parent or an educator you may be feeling like you can't take on one more thing. You may be thinking about how hard it is to just do what is required of you as a parent trying to get through the responsibilities of daily life. To these sentiments, first, I would say that anything can be accomplished if done methodically in small bits. And secondly, I would say that you cannot afford to let less important things take precedence over this.

As a school or in a classroom perhaps you could have a monthly virtue that you focus on. From that virtue choose a short Scripture a week that supports that virtue. Post it in your classroom. Recite it every time you have a little break in between subjects, as you walk to a special class, as you wait in a dismissal line. I guarantee within a couple days most of your students will know it by heart. You could do the same thing with a four- or five-stanza poem that supports your virtue. If creative, you can find all those wasted moments of the day and fill them with meaningful recitation. For the other practical things such as math facts, history facts, etc., take one minute at the beginning of your lessons to recite out loud whatever it is they are learning. It's doable!

As a parent—apply the same priciples at home! Use the Scripture from school or have one you choose at home and say it together before you pray at a meal. Recite it as you say goodnight and say a prayer with your child at bedtime. Turn off the radio in your car and the TV in your home and spend a little time filling the minds of your children with such things as life-giving words, poetry, and music to strengthen their hearts for life! By doing this you will be fulfilling God's command:

> Hear, O Israel! The LORD is our God, the LORD alone! Therefore, you shall love the LORD, your God, with your whole heart, and with your whole being, and with your

3. Swindoll, "Memorizing Scripture."

whole strength. Take to heart these words which I command you today. Keep repeating them to your children.
Recite them when you are at home and when you are
away, when you lie down and when you get up. Bind
them on your arm as a sign and let them be as a pendant
on your forehead. Write them on the doorposts of your
houses and on your gates.

—Deuteronomy 6:4–9 (NRSV)

It's pretty clear, isn't it?

Reclaim the Teaching of History

As I am finishing up this book in October of 2017 I have found
myself pondering all the divisions of our time—political, racial,
ideological, moral, and the list goes on. There is a battle in the media, a struggle in the White House, violence in our world, natural
disasters, a mass shooting in Las Vegas, confusion over our identity as men and women, athletes taking a knee during our national
anthem, etc. These are confusing times, times in desperate need
of God, His Word, and His ways. All the more reason to shore up
our homes and our schools and fill them with faith, with God's
presence, His Word, with hope, and with love.

But also for the sake of our nation—I believe there is one
thing we have lost over the years and need to reclaim in our
schools. That one thing is a love for our nation! Our students
need to have knowledge of the foundation on which our nation
was built. They need to understand the principles upon which our
Constitution stands and the challenges to those principles we have
faced throughout the years. At the age of sixty I look back on my
education and can clearly see how the teaching of our American
story had begun to fade. There is so much I had never learned as
a child—one with thirteen years of Catholic education—and only
discovered when I opened that small Christian school and began to
dig for a Christian-based curriculum. It was then, for the students
in our school and personally for me, that I began to understand
and marvel at our story as a nation—at our Christian foundation,

and at the men and women who were so critical to that story. If we are ever to regain pride in our nation, hope in our founding principles, and strength to move forward for the sake of this next generation, we have to grow as people of prayer and people who know our heritage and understand the covenant made with God at the very beginnings of this nation, this experiment in democracy.

We must as Catholic schools return to a rich teaching of world and American history! We must make it a priority to share with our students the ideas and practices that destroyed nations and those ideals and principles that make a nation great. We must search for texts that are not altered and watered down to discredit our history, but texts true to that history even if they are old and dusty. Our students must have the opportunity to read and ponder those early documents and the words, perspectives, and inspiration of our Founding Fathers.

As stated by George Washington:

> A primary object should be the education of our youth in the science of government. In a republic, what species of knowledge can be equally important? And what duty more pressing than communicating it to those who are to be the future guardians of the liberties of the country?[4]

As I drive through the campus of the University of Michigan in Ann Arbor close to where I live and I read the inscriptions on the original buildings, I am in awe of the inspiring words of faith, but also deeply saddened how far that institution has strayed from those words—the case on so many university campuses. Did you know that 106 of the first 108 colleges in America were founded on our Christian faith? You would never know it now. Consider this from Harvard's *Rules and Precepts*, published September 26, 1642:

> Let every Student be plainly instructed, and earnestly pressed to consider well, the maine end of his life and studies is, to know God and Jesus Christ which is eternall life, John 17:3 and therefore to lay Christ in the bottome, as the only foundation of all sound knowledge and

---

4. Liles, "Get Ready for Presidents Day," #6.

Learning. And seeing the Lord only giveth wisedome,
Let every one seriously set himself by prayer in secret to
seeke it of him Prov. 2,3.[5]

It is now 2021, and just recently it was announced that Harvard's new chief chaplain is an atheist. God has been removed, voices are being silenced, and our youth are confused. We must arm them for the struggles ahead for them.

Again—I realize trying to recapture authentic teaching of world and American history will take some work. Unfortunately, there are not many places for a Catholic school to turn to for materials that are true and free from our modern culture's imprint, but educators are resourceful and with some digging and careful selecting it can be done! There is a wonderful work that began awhile back to address the problems found in secular texts called the Catholic Textbook Project. Here is an excerpt from their website:

> In the year 2000 a group of Catholic educators and writers first met to launch the Catholic Textbook Project. We gathered to address an urgent need—a lack of Catholic textbooks. Frustrated with the poor quality, sloppy scholarship, and anti-Catholic bias of secular textbooks, we knew something new needed to be done for the sake of Catholic students and the future of Catholic education. We took the bold step of founding a publishing company and began the first series of history books specifically produced for Catholic schools since the 1960s.[6]

Right now they have beautiful history texts for grades 4–12 with the hopes of publishing additional ones for the lower grades. They also stock excellent Christian-focused science texts for grades 6 through high school. There are other publishers (Catholic and Christian) with history materials to fill in the gap where needed. Please see the Resources page at the end of the book for a list of Catholic and Christian publishers I have found excellent through the years.

5. Federer, "Harvard."
6. Catholic Textbook Project, "About."

Curriculum

The careful choosing of curriculum in Catholic Schools is critical! We must guard the hearts of the children in our care by guarding everything we place before them. We all know that secular publishers are driven by the demands of the culture—a culture today which does not seem it could be any more anti-Christian than it is now.

Consider these words from an article titled "Secular Resources Can Be Dangerous to Catholic Education" written by Patrick Reilly in June of 2021:

> An education that ignores God withholds understanding from its students. The lack of catechesis is only part of the problem. Secular education restricts understanding in every course of study by eclipsing the light of the Church's teachings, and it allows distortions and falsehoods to creep into every classroom. While subjects can be taught without reference to God, the approach is backward and narrow, deliberately limiting a student's understanding of reality as fashioned by God according to His reason. Ignoring the truths of our faith implicitly denies the unity of knowledge, and it prevents a truly integrated education with God as the common thread.
>
> Concerning the role of theology in education, St. John Henry Newman asked, "How can we investigate any part of any order of knowledge, and stop short of that which enters into every order? All true principles run over with it, all phenomena converge to it; it is truly the First and the Last."
>
> Secular materials and programs in math, literature, and even virtue development may appear suitable to Catholic education, because they include much of the same content. But mission drives Catholic education before content. Catholic education forms young people to use their unique human gifts of reason, free will, and selfless charity toward the end for which they were created.
>
> Whereas secular education helps students accumulate information and perhaps even develop skills of reasoning, Catholic education "ascends" above

knowledge toward transcendental reality—another Newman insight—to better understand and appreciate God's truth, goodness, and beauty as found in creation and in the Church.

Ultimately, then, the gulf between secular and Catholic education is much wider than it may first seem, and secular resources are never as suitable as those designed with an authentic Catholic perspective. Only a faithful Catholic education can integrally form young people in both mind and soul, as God intends.

It is important that Catholic educators remain confident in the superior formation that a faithful Catholic education provides. Secular programs and materials should be examined cautiously, with a preference toward resources that are built upon a Catholic foundation.[7]

This Scripture verse is one that I always referred to as a guide to make important decisions as a principal in the Christian school and three Catholic schools I have served:

Finally, beloved, whatever is true, whatever is honorable, whatever is just, whatever is pure, whatever is pleasing, whatever is commendable, if there is any excellence and if there is anything worthy of praise, think about these things. Keep on doing the things that you have learned and received and heard and seen in me, and the God of peace will be with you.

—Phillipians 4:8–9 (NRSV)

These words were the measuring stick for curriculum, library books, programs, clubs, and activities within the schools where I worked. If something did not pass this test, it was not utilized in the school.

There are some who would say that children need to be exposed to opposing views and concerns in the culture so it can be discussed. In my opinion those topics and ideas need to be reserved for older students, maybe high school, then college, after many years of solid instruction in faith and virtue. Elementary and

7. Reilly, "Secular Resources Can Be Dangerous."

middle-school students should not be exposed by our schools to ideas and topics that contradict the Christian faith. We have the mission to educate them.

It is true that there are not nearly enough Catholic publishers out there, but there are more than there were five years ago. They may not have all the bells and whistles of secular books, but good, solid, faith-filled teachers do not need bells and whistles—they need truth. If you are willing to dig, you will find excellent curriculum for your students. Search for Catholic materials first and if you are coming up short in a specific area, look to solid Christian publishers. There really are excellent choices out there if you are willing to put in the effort to search and willing to combine the two where necessary.

So—these are just a few additional areas I think we really need to consider addressing in our schools. We need to stop chasing after all the latest and greatest new advances in education and prayerfully consider what "tried-and-true" approaches from the past need to be resurrected and given a place of prominence in our schools and homes.

Final Thoughts

May the God of hope fill you with all joy and peace in believing, so that you may abound in hope by the power of the Holy Spirit.

—ROMANS 15:13 (NRSV)

I FIND MYSELF HERE at the end of this journey of sharing my thoughts and perspectives about Catholic education. As I pondered what else I might feel was left unsaid in the book and what I wanted to be the final words of this collection of thoughts I found the above Scripture perfect. We have hope!

As I shared, some of the writing I did for this book was in the midst of the 2016 presidential election. I am now preparing to send this book off for publishing in September of 2021 and could never have imagined then what we would be in the midst of now. Every day that we turn on the news we hear about division, fear, attacks, protests, distrust, scandals, and the loss of some personal freedoms. We have spent the last year-and-a-half living in the midst of the COVID-19 pandemic. I lost my brother to this virus in the early days of its arrival, and my life at times has felt almost surreal. The isolation, loneliness, and uncertainty have been extremely difficult to navigate for everyone, including our precious children. We can become overwhelmed by it all and wonder if normalcy, civility, and a sense of pride in our nation will ever return.

And most importantly we can begin to wonder if trust in God will ever be a part of the fabric of our nation again.

Because of all this craziness and uncertainty, our Catholic churches, homes, and schools are essential to restoring a sense of faith and hope in our society. Our Catholic schools have a very challenging but amazing opportunity to work towards turning despair into hope, fear into trust, and hate into love. The children that walk through the doors of our Catholic schools each day do so oftentimes with heavy burdens and without a sense of God's amazing love for them. If we respond only by providing an excellent education, we will have failed them greatly. These children, through no fault of their own, are bombarded by so much that is out of their control, a constantly changing pandemic, overscheduled lives, technology overload, and a lack of quiet and reflection. As a result, they have been robbed of the freedom and innocence childhood should provide, robbed of genuine pure joy.

Recognizing this should prompt a very intentional response in our homes and the organization and planning of our schools. Knowing this should stir continual discussion about the atmosphere of our schools. We should be asking ourselves if, as schools, we can provide some of what has been stolen from them. How will we guide them to a living relationship with Jesus Christ? How will we show them in practical and less obvious ways that they can have a very personal, vibrant relationship with Christ and that the power of the Holy Spirit is accessible to them? How can we create a school atmosphere that welcomes God into everything?

Can we help them develop a sincere prayer life? Can prayer be so central to our days in school that these children learn that it is the first response to any problem, doubt, or fear? Can they trust that the adults around them will guide them to prayer in big and small ways all throughout the day and teach them to cast every burden on God? Will they be taught how important it is to pray for one another, their families, our Church, and our nation?

Will we teach them to worship? Will we take the time to plan Masses and other practices such as Stations of the Cross, May Crowning, etc., in a way that touches their senses and reaches deep into their hearts? Will we teach them that their life, their school-work, their play, everything they do is a form of worship to God? Will we fill our halls and classrooms with beautiful sacred art to inspire their minds to rise to loftier thoughts?

Will we restore joy to them? Will we be intentional about creating joyful, vibrant schools? Will we begin and end our days in prayer? Will we fill our halls with uplifting, faith-filled music as the day begins, throughout the day in classrooms, and as the day ends, knowing that music touches the soul in ways that nothing else can?

Will there be laughter and a lightheartedness in our schools? Will we look for ways to celebrate together and teach them that at times you need to put other things aside to share in joy together?

Will we pay attention to the signs of our times and do every-thing in our power to give the students in our care an environment that they may only be able to experience while they are at school? Will we help parents see the need for slowing down and encour-age them to pay attention to the condition of our society? Will we have the courage to put natural barriers in place to help families experience a Sabbath by avoiding things like athletic practices and games on Sundays? Will we have the guts to challenge parents to put their hope in God rather than media, traveling teams, and a social calendar that does nothing more than add busyness and stress to their lives?

These are all questions that each school and church will have to ask itself. Every situation is different and needs honest discus-sion relevant to that specific community. I will say, though, that if we don't ask the questions now, if we put it off until another time or pass it on to someone else to deal with, we will have missed the signs of the times and the opportunity to begin trying to straighten the course for this generation and the ones to follow. Another gen-eration of children and grandchildren will be lost to the pressures of the culture.

These are unprecedented times that require courage, boldness, and great faith! It is not time for three- or five-year plans—that is not fair to those in need right now. It is not time to throw up our hands in defeat, but instead to draw closer to Christ and trust that

He will not fail us! We must be intentional and persevere, drawing wisdom from the words of Mother Teresa: "Yesterday is gone; tomorrow has not yet come. We have only today. Let us begin."[1]

Finally, consider these words from Scripture:

> Therefore, since it is by God's mercy that we are engaged in this ministry, we do not lose heart. We have renounced the shameful things that one hides; we refuse to practice cunning or to falsify God's word; but by the open statement of the truth we commend ourselves to the conscience of everyone in the sight of God. And even if our gospel is veiled, it is veiled to those who are perishing. In their case the god of this world has blinded the minds of the unbelievers, to keep them from seeing the light of the gospel of the glory of Christ, who is the image of God. For we do not proclaim ourselves; we proclaim Jesus Christ as Lord and ourselves as your slaves for Jesus' sake. For it is the God who said, "Let light shine out of darkness," who has shone in our hearts to give the light of the knowledge of the glory of God in the face of Jesus Christ.
>
> But we have this treasure in clay jars, so that it may be made clear that this extraordinary power belongs to God and does not come from us. We are afflicted in every way, but not crushed; perplexed, but not driven to despair; persecuted, but not forsaken; struck down, but not destroyed; always carrying in the body the death of Jesus, so that the life of Jesus may also be made visible in our bodies. For while we live, we are always being given up to death for Jesus' sake, so that the life of Jesus may be made visible in our mortal flesh. So death is at work in us, but life in you.
>
> But just as we have the same spirit of faith that is in accordance with scripture—"I believed, and so I spoke"—we also believe, and so we speak, because we know that the one who raised the Lord Jesus will raise us also with Jesus, and will bring us with you into His presence. Yes, everything is for your sake, so that grace, as it extends to more and more people, may increase thanksgiving, to the glory of God.

---

1. Teresa, *In the Heart of the World*, 17.

So we do not lose heart. Even though our outer nature is wasting away, our inner nature is being renewed day by day. For this slight momentary affliction is preparing us for an eternal weight of glory beyond all measure, because we look not at what can be seen but at what cannot be seen; for what can be seen is temporary, but what cannot be seen is eternal.

—2 Corinthians 4:1–18 (NRSV)

You see, we can no longer be nice little schools providing a better-than-average education. We have a commission to open our eyes, put aside our pride, recognize where we have failed, and make a decision to respond!

Will you?

Suggested Resources to Consider

This is but a small list of some of my favorites to get you started—there are many more wonderful resources available—you just have to dig!

Curriculum

- The Catholic Textbook Project—history grades 4–12, science grades 6–12.
  https://www.catholictextbookproject.com

- Seton Educational Media—see history for grades K–4.
  https://setonbooks.com

- Mother of Divine Grace—see curriculum overview for recommendations.
  https://modg.org/curriculum

- Memoria Press—curriculum for every subject—note especially literature.
  https://www.memoriapress.com

- ABeka—rigorous Christian curriculum—grades PreK–12.
  https://www.abeka.com

- Easy Grammar—solid grammar program for grades 1–12+.
  https://www.easygrammar.com/store/c1/Featured_Products.html

- Saxon Math—solid spiral math curriculum.
  https://www.hmhco.com/programs/saxon-math#overview

- 102 Top Picks for Homeschool Curriculum—Cathy Duffy—Don't be deterred by the term "homeschool." https://cathyduffyreviews.com/homeschool-extras/parent-helps-and-how-to-books/general-parent-helps/102-top-picks-for-homeschool-curriculum

Catholic Faith

- Faith and Life—solid and strong instruction in faith grades 1–8—beautiful artwork. https://www.ignatius.com/promotions/faithandlife/

- Open Light Media—Sisters of Mary Mother of the Eucharist—virtue program. https://openlightmedia.com

- Ruah Woods Press—theology of the body, K–12 curriculum. https://www.ruahwoodspress.com

- Good News Book Fair—Catholic book fair materials. https://www.goodnewsbookfair.com

- Ignatius Press—Catholic book club, Catholic movie nights. https://ignatiusbookclub.com https://www.ignatius.com/promotions/movienights/

- Donut Man—excellent Christian and Catholic songs for young children. Many of his songs are available on YouTube as well as through Integrity music. http://www.donutman.streamlinenettrial.co.uk

Parents

- J. C. Ryle, *The Duties of Parents*—excellent short but powerful book about parenting in faith. https://www.amazon.com/Duties-Parents-J-C-Ryle/dp/1481240803

Bibliography

Augustine of Hippo. *Confessions of Saint Augustine.* https://www.gutenberg.
org/files/3296/3296-h/3296-h.htm.

Benedict XVI, Pope. *Deus Caritas Est.* https://www.vatican.va/content/
benedict-xvi/en/encyclicals/documents/hf_ben-xvi_enc_20051225_
deus-caritas-est.html.

————. *Pastoral Visit of His Holiness Pope Benedict XVI in Poland: Address
by the Holy Father: Meeting With the Clergy.* https://www.vatican.va/
content/benedict-xvi/en/speeches/2006/may/documents/hf_ben-xvi_
spe_20060525_poland-clergy.html.

Byers, Gary. "The Lesson of the Lamp." *Associates for Biblical Research*, August
26, 2014. https://biblearchaeology.org/research/devotionals/4131-the-
lesson-of-the-lamp.

Catechism of the Catholic Church. 2nd ed. https://www.vatican.va/archive/
ENG0015/_INDEX.HTM.

Catholic Textbook Project. "About." https://www.catholictextbookproject.com/
about.

De Souza, Raymond J. "Why Are So Many of the Professional Jobs in the
Church Held by Dissidents?" *LifeSite*, November 26, 2010. https://www.
lifesitenews.com/blogs/wh,y-are-so-many-of-the-professional-jobs-in-
the-church-held-by-dissidents.

Eberle, Gary. *Sacred Time and the Search for Meaning.* Berkeley, CA: Shambala,
2002.

Federer, Bill. "Harvard: American Minute With Bill Federer." *The Good News
Today*, October 2018. https://thegoodnewstoday.org/harvard/.

Fenelon, Marge. "The Power of Novenas." *Our Sunday Visitor*, April 30, 2014.
https://osvnews.com/2014/04/30/the-power-of-novenas/.

Francis, Pope. *The Joy of Discipleship: Reflections From Pope Francis on Walking
with Christ.* Chicago, IL: Loyola, 2016.

Goodman, Allegra. "And on the Seventh Day, She Rests: Hardworking Modern
Woman Celebrates the Restorative Power of the Sabbath." *Real Simple*,
March 2001.

Guest, Edgar Albert. "Don't Quit." http://faculty.wiu.edu/M-Cole/Paige+Poems. pdf.

IgnatianSpirituality.com. "The Daily Examen." https://www.ignatianspirituality. com/ignatian-prayer/the-examen/.

John Paul II, Pope. *15th World Youth Day Address of the Holy Father John Paul II: Vigil of Prayer*. https://www.vatican.va/content/john-paul-ii/en/ speeches/2000/jul-sep/documents/hf_jp-ii_spe_20000819_gmg-veglia. html.

———. *Letter on the 75th Anniversary of the Feast of Corpus Christi #8. CatholicSaints.Info*, May 28, 1996. https://catholicsaints.info/pope-john-paul-ii-letter-on-the-750th-anniversary-of-the-feast-of-corpus-christi-28-may-1996/.

Laurie, Greg. "What Every Believer Should Know about Backsliding." *LightSource*. https: www.lightsource.com/ministry/greg-laurie-tv/articles/ what-every-believer-should-know-about-backsliding-12562.html.

Liles, Marilyn. "Get Ready for Presidents Day with 125 Quotes from George Washington." *Parade.com*, February 1, 2021. https://parade.com/989259/ marynliles/george-washington-quotes/.

Longenecker, Dwight. "Why Don't Catholics Read The Bible?" November 17, 2015. https://dwightlongenecker.com/why-dont-catholics-read-the-bible/.

Marketing Charts. "Social Networking Eats Up 3+ Hours per Day for the Average American User." https://www.marketingcharts.com/digital-26049.

McFarlane, Bud. *A Bright Future for the Catholic Church in America*. Fairview Park, OH: Mary Foundation, 2013. https://www.catholicity.com/booklets/ future.pdf.

McKinney, Charlie. "The Effects of Holy Water." *SpiritualDirection.com*, October 11, 2017. https://spiritualdirection.com/2017/10/11/the-effects-of-holy-water.

Miller, J. Michael. "The Holy See's Teaching on Catholic Schools—The Catholic University of America." *Catholic Education Resource Center*, September 14, 2005. https://www.catholiceducation.org/en/education/catholic-contributions/the-holy-sees-teaching-on-catholic-schools.html.

Paul VI, Pope. *Mysterium Fidei*. https://www.vatican.va/content/paul-vi/en/ encyclicals/documents/hf_p-vi_enc_03091965_mysterium.html.

Reilly, Patrick. "Secular Resources Can Be Dangerous to Catholic Education." *The Cardinal Newman Society*, June 28, 2021. https://newmansociety.org/ secular-resources-can-be-dangerous-to-catholic-education/.

Stanley, Bob. "The Power of Holy Water." https://www.thecatholictreasurechest. com/holywatr.htm.

Swindoll, Chuck. "Memorizing Scripture." *Insight for Today*, September 26, 2015. https://www.insight.org/resources/daily-devotional/individual/ memorizing-scripture.

Teresa, Mother. *In the Heart of the World: Thoughts, Stories, & Prayers*. Novato, CA: New World Library, 2010.

Bibliography

Turley, K. V. "Hidden Power of Holy Water." *Catholic Exchange*, February 16, 2017. https://catholicexchange.com/hidden-power-holy-water.

TutorHunt. "In Praise of Memorization: 10 Proven Brain Benefits." https://www.tutorhunt.com/resource/22593/blog/in-praise-of-memorization-10-proven-brain-benefits/.

Vatican Radio. "Pope sends message for Italy's upcoming Eucharistic Congress." *Vatican Radio*, July 7, 2016. http://www.archivioradiovaticana.va/storico/2016/07/07/pope_sends_message_for_italy's_upcoming_eucharistic_congress/en-1242541.

Webster, Noah. *An American Dictionary of the Engish Language, 1828*. San Francisco: Foundation for American Christian Education, 1989.

CPSIA information can be obtained
at www.ICGtesting.com
Printed in the USA
BVHW031741040622
638933BV00004B/42

9 781666 734577